The Etruscans

Ellen Macnamara

HARVARD UNIVERSITY PRESS

Cambridge, Massachusetts

1991

**To my niece
FRANCES ELLEN
ROBERTSON**

THIS PAGE View of Orvieto from
the south-west. Situated upon an
almost impregnable plateau, the
city dominates the valleys of the
Paglia and the Chiana. Its
importance in Etruscan times is
attested by the remains of the
temples within its walls and
extensive cemeteries on the flanks
of the plateau.

**Illustration
acknowledgements**

Ellen Macnamara: pp.2–3, Figs
2, 15, 18. T. Rasmussen: Fig.
12. Pubbli Aer Foto. Milan: Fig.
11. Hirmer Fotoarchiv,
Munich: Figs 36, 37, 50, 51.
Università di Roma 'La
Sapienza', Dipartimento di
scienze storiche archeologiche e
antropologiche dell'antichità:
Museo di antichità etrusche e
italiche (photo M. Bellisario):
Fig. 19. Fig. 17 is from
A. Boëthius, *Etruscan and Early
Roman Architecture*, fig. 82. Figs
3 and 9 are by Susan Bird and
Susan Goddard. Figs 5 and 16
are drawn by Susan Bird from
E. Macnamara, *Everyday Life of
the Etruscans*, figs 3 and 23. Fig.
56 is drawn by Eva Wilson
from E. Macnamara, op. cit.,
fig. 72. Fig. 78 is drawn by
Susan Bird from M. Pallottino,
The Etruscans, fig. 6.

Acknowledgements

First I would like to thank Brian Cook, Keeper of the Department of Greek and
Roman Antiquities, for asking me to write this book and, together with my
colleague, Judith Swaddling, for reading the draft text and greatly improving it.
I am also pleased to acknowledge Andrew Burnett's advice upon Etruscan coins
and Larissa Bonfante's guidance on Etruscan inscriptions.

I am deeply grateful to my friends and colleagues in Etruscan studies, Sybille
Haynes, Francesca and David Ridgway and Fiona Campbell, for reading and
correcting my script. Any mistakes which have survived their careful comments
are my own.

I wish to thank most warmly many colleagues in the British Museum, without
whose help this book could not have been achieved. In particular, I would like to
mention Susan Bird and Susan Goddard for the maps and other drawings, and
Eva Wilson for her wash drawing. Christi Graham and P. E. Nicholls are
responsible for the splendid photographs and I am very grateful for their skill and
care. I also wish to record my gratitude to Bernard Jackson and Roger Flint for
their help in organising the photographs and to Lloyd Gallimore, Kim Overend,
Emma Cox and Susan Smith, the Museum Assistants who helped so much in
assembling the objects for photography.

Finally, I wish to thank Celia Clear of British Museum Publications for her
encouragement, and to record my sincere gratitude to Teresa Francis, my editor,
for her expertise and patience.

ELLEN MACNAMARA
December 1989

Contents

Preface

This small book is intended to serve both as a general introduction to Etruscan civilisation and as a companion commentary on the exhibition of Etruscan objects in the gallery of the British Museum entitled 'Italy before the Roman Empire'. There may be said to be three main phases in the acquisition of the British Museum's Etruscan collection. First, there are the rich assemblages either presented by or bought from British and foreign antiquarians and collectors of the eighteenth and early nineteenth centuries. Outstanding among these scholars were Sir William Hamilton, who from 1764 to 1800 was the British diplomatic representative at Naples; Charles Townley and Richard Payne Knight, both of whom travelled and collected in Italy towards the end of the eighteenth century, and later the Hon. Sir William Temple, who was British Ambassador in Naples during the early nineteenth century.

The second phase began with the period of the greatest exploitation of the cemeteries of ancient Etruria after 1828; in that year a tomb with rich contents was accidentally discovered near Vulci on the property of Lucien Bonaparte, Prince of Canino. Subsequently, a vast number of other tombs were found on this estate; only objects considered to be of value were kept and these were sold in the following years. Some were acquired by the British Museum

at one of Canino's sales; others, like the objects said to be from the 'Isis Tomb' of the Polledrara cemetery at Vulci, entered the collection indirectly through the hands of dealers. Canino's activities at Vulci were soon followed by those of the Campanari family of Tuscania, who found and removed the contents of many undisturbed tombs but also did much to introduce the Etruscans to a wide European public. In 1837, Carlo Campanari organised the first exhibition of Etruscan antiquities ever held in Britain; it took place in a house in Pall Mall, London, where rooms were arranged to resemble Etruscan tombs with replicas of wall-paintings or with sarcophagi, some with their lids left slightly open to reveal a skeleton, and the walls hung with vases and bronze utensils. Many of the objects in this exhibition were bought by the British Museum, which continued to acquire further groups from the Campanari family until 1849.

The Pall Mall exhibition evoked much public interest in the Etruscans and shortly afterwards, between the years 1842 and 1847, an Englishman, George Dennis, travelled widely throughout Etruria, with the intention of writing a book of 'truth and accuracy' upon Etruscan places and civilisation. He achieved this in his great work *The Cities and Cemeteries of Etruria*, which was first published in 1848 and remains a valuable source of information to this day. Dennis was sometimes accompanied on his travels by Samuel James Ainsley, a gifted artist, who carefully sketched many Etruscan sites. He bequeathed his works to the British Museum and several are illustrated in this book.

Intact tombs must have continued to be found in considerable numbers throughout Etruria during the second half of the nineteenth century, with a lively local appreciation of the worth of their contents, and in Britain public interest must have remained high, for the British Museum bought several large series of acquisitions from the Castellani family between 1865 and 1884. The Castellani family firm specialised in the adaptation and reproduction of ancient jewellery but they also collected and traded in antiquities; an astonishing number of

Etruscan objects reached the British Museum from this family, mainly from Alessandro Castellani.

After this, the third phase is characterised by a smaller but steady acquisition of Etruscan objects from a wide number of sources. Notable groups include those from the collections of Sir A.W. Franks and Captain E.G. Spencer-Churchill, the former assembled in the late nineteenth century and the latter during the current century.

The Etruscan collection in the British Museum includes many outstanding objects and is remarkably comprehensive; with the exception of wall-paintings from tombs, it is an assembly fully capable of reflecting the broad stream of Etruscan civilisation. Thus, when considering the purpose of this book and mindful of the many excellent books on Etruscan art now in print, the author decided not to reproduce much-published masterpieces of Etruscan art in museums round the world but rather to take the opportunity to illustrate as wide a variety as possible of the Etruscan objects in the British Museum, while mentioning others in the text. In this way, it is hoped that this book will provide not only a useful commentary and lasting memento for visitors to the exhibition of the Etruscan collection in the British Museum, but also encourage readers to travel in ancient Etruria and visit other museums with an increased understanding of Etruscan civilisation.

NOTES

1 It is impossible to be consistent in the usage of place-names in this book, but it is hoped that a general clarity has been achieved. Modern Italian place-names are used with their Greek or Latin equivalents in brackets beside them, where this has seemed necessary, and the ancient name where the sense demanded it. English names for Italian cities are used when they are very familiar to speakers of English.

2 The names commonly given to Etruscan tombs are sometimes descriptive, sometimes given to honour the discoverer or owner, and occasionally local nicknames. English translations are used in this book whenever possible.

1 Geography and Archaeological Background

Ancient Etruria, the heartland of the Etruscan people, lay in west central Italy and was bounded to the north by the valley of the Arno, to the east and south by the Tiber and to the west by the Tyrrhenian Sea, where the Etruscans held the small off-shore islands, including Elba. This area may roughly be compared with the size of Wales. In the course of their history, the Etruscans settled colonies as far south as Campania, to the north over the Apennines in the lower Po Valley and on Corsica. Memory of the Etruscan period is still recalled in some modern place-names, that of the Tyrrhenian Sea deriving from the Greek name for the Etruscans, the Tyrrhenians, and that of Tuscany from the Latin, for the Romans called the Etruscans Tusci or Etrusci. They called themselves Rasenna.

The geology of ancient Etruria may broadly be divided into southern and northern regions. Generally the rocks of the southern area are of volcanic origin, often the soft rock termed 'tuff', which is formed of the layers of ash flung from the volcanoes whose craters now form the lakes of Bolsena, Vico and Bracciano. With the exception of some rocks of an older geological formation, this area is characterised by a broad coastal plain and a rolling upland plateau, which is intersected by the valleys and ravines cut by rivers and streams. These drain into the Tiber or westwards into the sea, and their valleys provided good internal routes of communication. The northern region is mainly formed of sandstones and limestones and may be subdivided into a western and an eastern area. The landscape to the west is almost mountainous, with hills reaching down to the coast and valleys draining north to the Arno or west to the sea. The eastern and inland area has a less rugged aspect and includes the broad, alluvial valleys of the upper Tiber and its tributaries, which surround the great lake of Trasimeno.

The rocks of Etruria were rich in minerals, with major resources of copper, tin, lead, silver and iron ores. The ore-bearing zones lay in

1 Drawing by S. J. Ainsley (1806–74) of the Lake of Bolsena. The lake lies in the volcanic region of southern Etruria, within an extinct crater.

2 View from the south-east of the site of Vetulonia, which crowns a steep-sided hill rising from the coastal plain.

OPPOSITE
3 Maps of the Mediterranean region and central Mediterranean area.

western and often coastal Etruria, principally around the Tolfa Hills, Monte Amiata, among the Colline Metallifere and on Elba.

The broad valleys of the Arno and the Tiber with their navigable rivers set natural geographical limits to Etruria, often defining political boundaries while at the same time providing easy routes of communication which united the Etruscans with their neighbours. Beyond these valleys to the north and east lies the range of the Apennines, which forms the curving spine of peninsular Italy. This was a formidable barrier in antiquity, though the small river valleys of the tributaries of the upper Arno and the lower Po were possible links with the north. To the south across the Tiber, the coastal plain of ancient Latium was accessible, while the easiest land route to Campania lay inland along the valleys of the Sacco and the Liri. Though natural deep-water harbours were absent from the coast of Etruria, prominent headlands, the mouths of rivers and coastal lagoons, now silted up, formed sheltered anchorages: open beaches, upon which boats could be pulled out of the water, often sufficed for ancient shipping. The early Etruscans were famous sailors and the sea provided them with the opportunity of contact and trade with other peoples of the Mediterranean.

The climate of Etruria was very favourable, and this is reflected in the many references of authors in antiquity to the fine forests and rich agricultural produce of the region. The forests had a wide variety of trees, notably oak, beech, chestnut and pine, which were required for the building of temples, houses, bridges and ships, as well as for making a multitude of objects on a smaller scale. The farmlands of Etruria, with their good soil and moderate rainfall and temperature, provided a good yield of fine grain, grapes, olives and other crops, including flax for linen. The Etruscans stocked cattle, sheep, goats, pigs and poultry, while there can be little doubt that the hunting of wild birds and animals, such

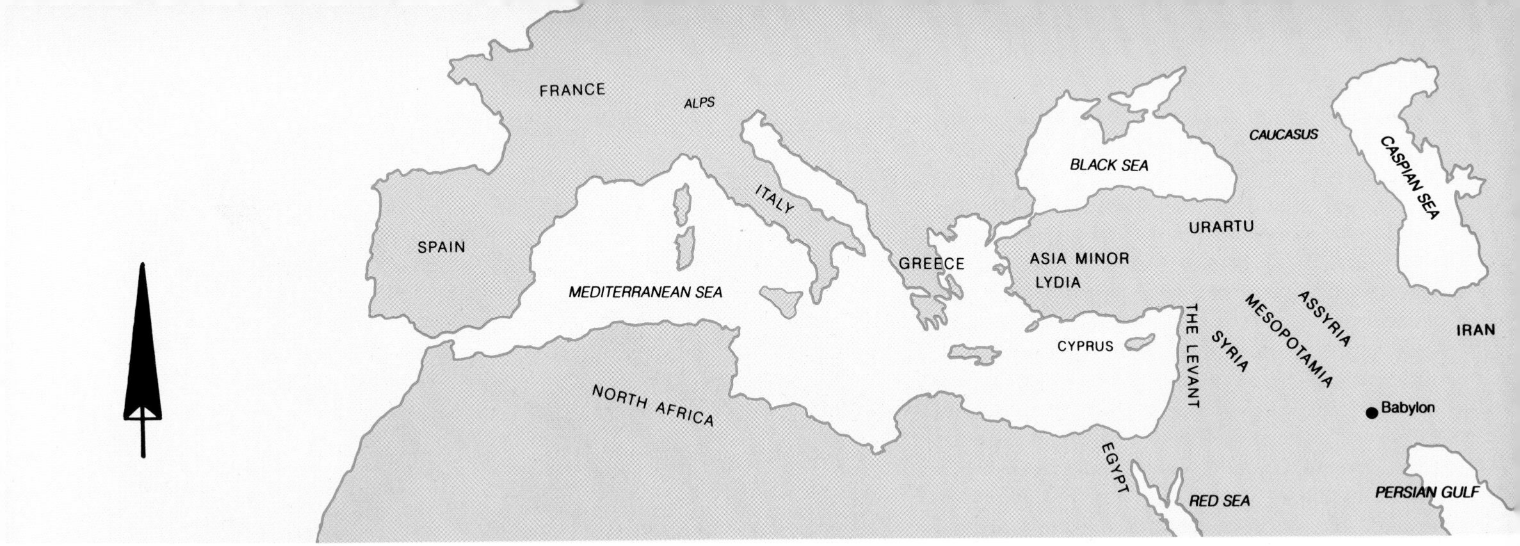
FRANCE
ALPS
SPAIN
ITALY
MEDITERRANEAN SEA
GREECE
NORTH AFRICA
BLACK SEA
CAUCASUS
CASPIAN SEA
URARTU
ASIA MINOR
LYDIA
CYPRUS
THE LEVANT
SYRIA
MESOPOTAMIA
ASSYRIA
IRAN
Babylon
EGYPT
RED SEA
PERSIAN GULF

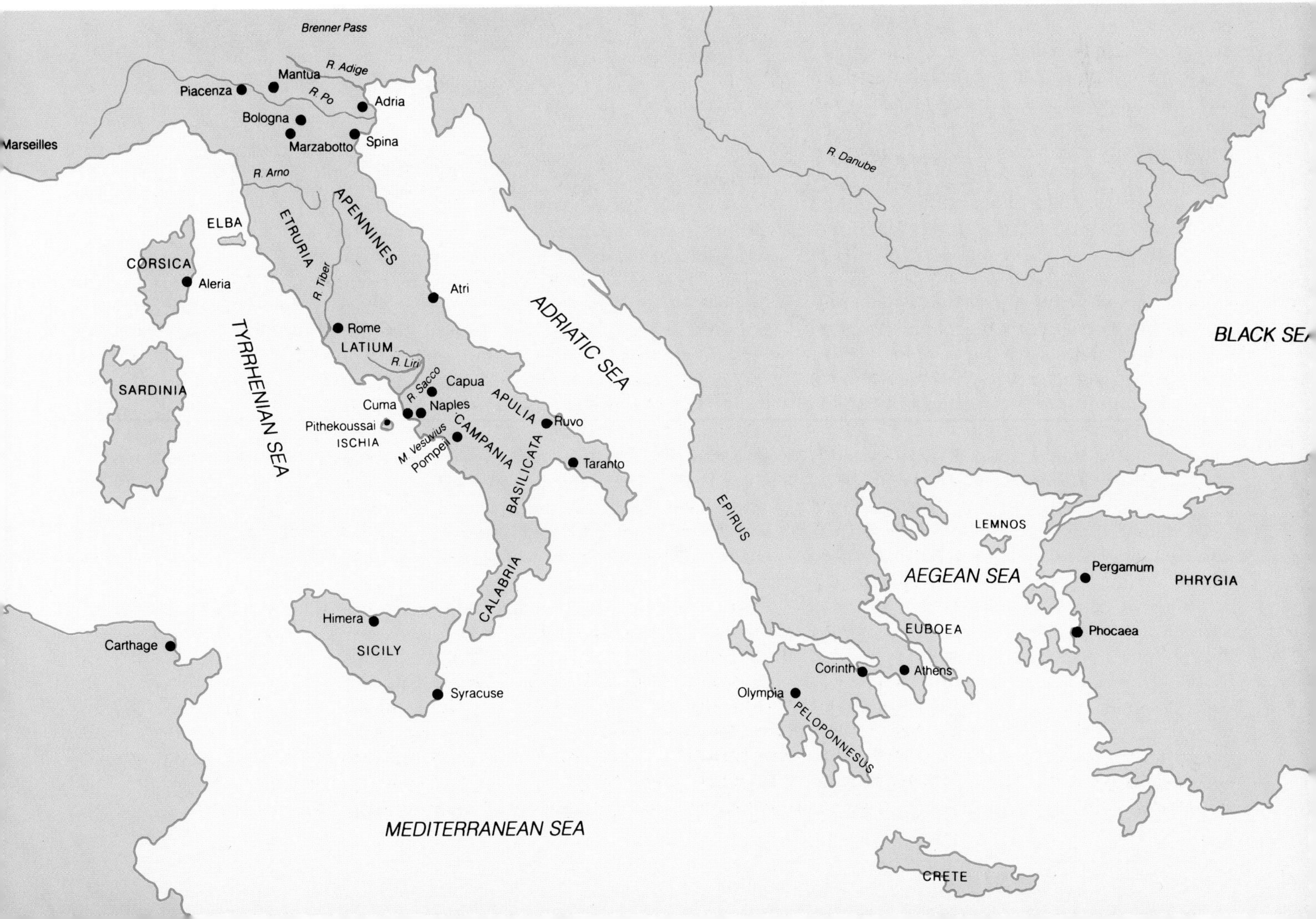
Brenner Pass
R. Adige
Mantua
Piacenza
R. Po
Adria
Bologna
Marzabotto
Spina
Marseilles
R. Arno
R. Danube
ELBA
ETRURIA
APENNINES
CORSICA
Aleria
R. Tiber
Atri
ADRIATIC SEA
Rome
LATIUM
TYRRHENIAN SEA
R. Liri
R. Sacco
Capua
SARDINIA
Cuma
Naples
APULIA
Ruvo
Pithekoussai
ISCHIA
M. Vesuvius
Pompeii
CAMPANIA
BASILICATA
Taranto
BLACK SEA
EPIRUS
LEMNOS
AEGEAN SEA
Pergamum
PHRYGIA
CALABRIA
Himera
SICILY
Carthage
Syracuse
EUBOEA
Phocaea
Corinth
Athens
Olympia
PELOPONNESUS
MEDITERRANEAN SEA
CRETE

as deer and boar, contributed to their subsistence, as did the fish caught in the rivers, lakes and sea.

Though favourable to settlement, Etruria was still quite sparsely populated during the Italian Early and Middle Bronze Ages (c. 2000–1250 BC) but local metal ores were already exploited. Towards the end of this period, mainland Greece was enjoying the sophisticated Mycenaean civilisation and there is much evidence that Mycenaean Greeks, as well as people from Crete and Cyprus, voyaged and traded widely in the west Mediterranean seas, probably in search of metal ores, including copper and tin, the alloys required for the manufacture of tin-bronze, and other rare commodities such as amber from the Baltic. After the fall of the Mycenaean civilisation and the disasters which occurred in the east Mediterranean region during the late thirteenth and twelfth centuries BC, most contacts between the east and west Mediterranean ceased, and during the latter part of the Italian Late Bronze Age (c. 1250–900 BC) many innovations in Italy stemmed from the flourishing cultures of central Europe and from east of the Adriatic Sea. Before the thirteenth century BC, the early peoples of Italy had generally buried their dead, laying them in many differing types of individual grave or collective tombs, but the custom of cremation and placing the ashes of the dead in cinerary urns grouped in cemeteries or urn-fields entered Italy from the north at this time and later became dominant in several regions.

Though iron was known, it was sparingly used during the Italian Early Iron Age (c. 900–700 BC), and many tools and weapons continued to be made of bronze. These centuries in Etruria are often termed the Villanovan period, a name adopted by modern archaeologists from the site of Villanova near Bologna, where this Italian Early Iron Age culture was first recognised during the last century. It should be emphasised that the modern use of the term 'Villanovan culture' simply describes the archaeological culture, or assemblage of similar material objects and identifiable social practices which are consistently found together, during the Italian Early Iron Age and mainly in the lower Po Valley to

the south of the River Po, in Etruria and in parts of Campania. It does not imply the existence of a distinct racial group and it is incorrect and misleading to call the Early Iron Age inhabitants of these regions 'the Villanovans'. The frequent use in modern literature of the term 'the Villanovans' has led to many confusions concerning early development in Etruria. Most important of these confusions has been the apparent discontinuity between the 'Villanovans' of the ninth and eighth centuries BC and the Etruscans of the seventh and subsequent centuries BC, when we know the Etruscan language was spoken in the region. This modern nomenclature has often been taken to imply an invasion of people and a change of language in Etruria around 700 BC. It cannot be stated too strongly that the many changes which took place in Etruria around that date are fully explained by the new contacts then established with the Greek world and the high cultures of the east Mediterranean regions and their colonial settlements in Italy. The fundamental cultural continuity between the ninth, eighth and seventh centuries in Etruria makes it certain that the Early Iron Age people were the true precursors of Etruscan civilisation and that

4a (*left*) Cinerary urn in the form of a hut. The urn represents a dwelling built of wooden posts and beams, with wattle and daub walls; poles laid across the roof hold the thatch in position. The door is placed below the gable, with a smoke-vent above. From the Alban Hills, Latium, 900–800 BC. H. 33 cm.

b (*right*) Cinerary urn of the Villanovan period, made of unrefined clay fired brown/black. It is biconical in form, with one handle, and has incised geometric decoration. 900–800 BC. H. 36 cm.

the inhabitants of Etruria during the Villanovan period were proto-Etruscans.

The Early Iron Age people of Etruria during the Villanovan period usually inhabited quite small villages. These villages were often grouped upon defensible sites, which were to become Etruscan towns or cities. They lived in oval or rectilinear huts, whose ground-plans with their post-holes have frequently been found and whose building techniques and appearance may be deduced from excavation and from the pottery models which were sometimes used as cinerary urns. They practised the funerary rite of cremation, burning the dead on pyres and placing their ashes in pottery or bronze cinerary urns, which were set in round pits or well-graves within a cemetery adjacent to the settlement.

The people of the Villanovan period often placed the prized possessions of the dead in their graves, and these objects not only help to date the individual grave-groups and allow us to comment upon their social system but also provide evidence for the contacts between the inhabitants of Etruria and the other peoples of Italy or further afield. At first, the graves show no great distinction of wealth, and women were often as richly equipped as men. Among luxury goods, the people of the Villanovan period had amber and glass and occasionally used precious metals for their jewellery, though this continued to be mainly made of bronze. Their pottery includes a wide variety of shapes, largely derived from Italian Bronze Age traditions; most of it was made of unrefined clay, formed without a potter's wheel, fired brown/black and sometimes burnished or decorated with geometric designs. Bronze was both cast and hammered, and bronze objects were embellished with incised and repoussé patterns. The bronze objects show a sustained influence from central Europe, but also the great strength of the regional Italian bronzeworking traditions at this time. One important link demonstrated by the distribution of bronze objects was the coastal trade already established in the ninth century BC between Sicily, Calabria, Campania and Etruria, while there is also much evidence for sea trade between Etruria, Sardinia and further afield in the

5 Drawing of a 'well-grave' (*pozzetto*) of the Villanovan period. A pottery vessel or urn for the ashes of the dead is placed in a small round pit cut into the rock and lined with stones above. 900–700 BC.

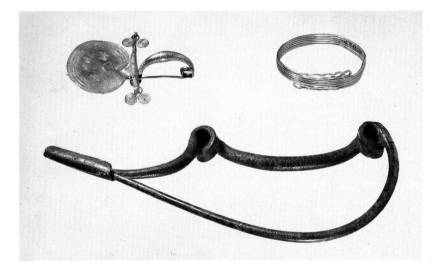

6 Gold and bronze jewellery of the Villanovan period:

a (*top left*) Gold brooch (*fibula*), its disc decorated with geometric patterns. If authentic, c.800 BC. L. 7.4 cm.

b (*top right*) Gold hair-ring or earring formed of coils of hammered wire, ending in a series of undulations. From Tarquinia, 800–700 BC. D. 5 cm.

c (*bottom*) Bronze fibula with an incised bow with two coils. The type is principally found in the west of Italy, from Sicily to Etruria, and was usually worn by men. 900–700 BC. L. 18.5 cm.

west Mediterranean area during the Villanovan period.

Early in the eighth century BC, trinkets from the east Mediterranean and Greek painted pottery begin to appear in Etruria, heralding new contacts with the east Mediterranean world. It is not yet clear exactly when Phoenicians from the great coastal cities of the Levant and Greeks first traded with Italy and then settled there during this colonial era, but the traditional date for the foundation of Carthage by the Phoenicians is 814 BC. Later, the Phoenicians and their successors the Carthaginian or Punic people placed colonies in western Sicily and on Sardinia. Ancient authors tell us that the first Greek settlement in Italy was the Euboean trading-post on Ischia, which the Greeks called Pithekoussai. Excavation on that island has confirmed that this took place by about 760 BC. Subsequently the entire southern coast of the peninsula from Taranto to Cuma, as well as the north-east, east and southern coast of Sicily, was settled with a chain of Greek colonies.

Both Phoenicians and Greeks must have been interested in the metal ores of Etruria, and it can be no coincidence that the first Greek trading-post in Italy was both furthest from Greece and closest to these resources. Indeed, contacts between the Euboean base on Ischia and Etruria are amply attested during the eighth century, both by imported pottery and even by the presence of Euboean Greeks working in the southern cities of Etruria. Such contacts, accompanied by the participation of other Greeks and Phoenicians, brought many innovations to Etruria, especially in the south. There was an increasing wealth and a greater social division exemplified by some rich graves of warriors, a growing use of iron particularly for tools and weapons, the advent of the potter's wheel and locally made pottery of purified, light-coloured fabric and painted decoration following Greek prototypes, as well as bronzes made in Etruria which imitated east Mediterranean and Greek models. The people of Etruria during the Villanovan period appear to have welcomed trade and new ideas, but in contrast to the inhabitants of Apulia, Basilicata, Calabria, Campania, Sicily and Sar-

dinia they must have been organised and strong enough to prevent any colonial encroachment upon their coastland; it may well be that their power at sea was a vital factor in this achievement. The fact that neither the Phoenicians nor the Greeks placed colonies in Etruria is of crucial significance in tracing the history of Etruscan civilisation and indeed that of Italy and western Europe.

No mention has yet been made of the vexed question of the 'origin of the Etruscans'. This question cannot be ignored, though it has rightly been declared that in studying Etruscan civilisation it is more constructive to describe its development down the centuries than to continue sterile speculations concerning this problem. There are three hypotheses concerning the origin of the Etruscans. According to a tradition well known in antiquity and mentioned in the fifth century BC by Herodotus (I, 94), the Etruscans migrated from Lydia in Asia Minor around the twelfth century BC, and surviving linguistic evidence shows that a dialect spoken during the sixth century BC on the island of Lemnos in the

7 Bronze equipment of the Villanovan period, with repoussé and incised decoration:

a (*top*) Crested helmet made from two hammered sheets. The type is derived from central European forms. Said to be from Vulci, 800–700 BC. H. 35 cm.

b (*right*) Cast sword with a hilt ending in a crescent-shaped pommel. The sheath is made of a folded bronze sheet, with a cast sphere at the tip. The type is found principally on the west coast of Italy, from Calabria to Etruria. 900–700 BC. L. 37 and 29.3 cm.

c (*bottom*) Oval facing for a leather belt, decorated with geometric patterns and birds. Such belts were often worn by women. 800–700 BC. L. 33 cm.

Aegean was similar to the Etruscan language. This linguistic evidence might be explained if the Etruscans brought their language from the Aegean area to Italy at an early date, or if it were a survival of a pre-Indo-European tongue once common around the Mediterranean. In the latter case, the Etruscans could have been an indigenous people of Italy, as was proposed by Dionysius of Halicarnassus (I, 28, 29 and 30) in the first century BC and is believed by many scholars today. Thirdly, it has been suggested that the Etruscans entered Italy from the north: this hypothesis principally rests upon similarities noted between the cultures of central Europe and the people of the Villanovan period in Italy during the early first millennium BC, and the evidence of inscriptions in Etruscan found in the valleys of the Alps. The former, however, may best be explained by trade, not migration, and the latter by the presence of Etruscan groups who fled into the mountains when the Gauls overran the Po Valley.

Thus the ethnic and linguistic affinities of the Etruscans are not yet clear, though it may be said that if a migration from the Aegean area did take place, it occurred before about 1000 BC. Some support for the memory of such an event among the Etruscans may be found in their reckoning of the *saecula* or 'centuries', which they believed were allotted by the gods for the time-span of their race. These uneven 'centuries' are mentioned by several Roman authors and, though their calculations differ, it seems that the Etruscans thought their first *saeculum* had started sometime during the eleventh or tenth century BC. At present, the archaeological evidence is less helpful than the study of linguistics in attempts to resolve the origin of the Etruscans, and it may be that further research on the relationship between Etruscan and other languages will shed more light on this problem.

8 Painted vases in Greek late Geometric tradition, probably made in southern Etruria:
a (*left*) Jar with basket-handle and two spouts, decorated with birds. The shape and decoration are in Euboean style and the jar, though perhaps made at Pithekoussai on Ischia, was most probably made in southern Etruria, 720–700 BC. H. 25 cm.
b (*right*) Jug (*oinochoe*) with several zones of decoration. The scene on the neck is perhaps the 'crane dance' performed by Theseus and Ariadne on Delos. Probably made by a Euboean Greek working in Etruria, perhaps at Tarquinia, 700–680 BC. H. 35 cm.

2 Cities, Tombs and Architecture

The evidence available from Etruscan places is still very uneven. Due to the lure of their rich contents, the cemeteries and tombs have attracted far more exploration, and exploitation, than have the settlements. Moreover, many Etruscan urban centres, and especially the inland cities, were continuously occupied throughout Roman and medieval times, as they are today; at these sites, Etruscan remains lie buried under later layers of building and, apart from city walls and adjacent cemeteries, only occasional glimpses of their presence may be found. On the other hand, where the site was abandoned in antiquity or during medieval times, it is now open to survey and excavation, and research has already demonstrated the wealth of available information and the potential for discoveries in the future. Most of these sites are in the coastal zone of Etruria, where malaria and piratical raids in lawless times, as well as the decline of local agriculture, must have contributed to the desertion of once-prosperous centres.

Probably as early as the eighth century BC, some of the village groups of the Villanovan period began to cohere into towns. These centres were often favoured by their defensible sites, their proximity to the source of metal ores or their position near important routes of communication, particularly those involved with the increasing trade with the Phoenicians and Greeks or their colonies in Italy. Gradually such towns came to dominate the neighbouring territory and to develop into the chief cities, or *metropoleis*, of the city-states, each with individual self-government, like those of the city states of Greece or the Greek colonies. At a time when the organisation of the Italian peoples was still mainly tribal, it may well be that the example of the Greek world influenced this development in Etruria, but demographic, social, economic and political factors must all have played a part. It is evident that this political system suited the contemporary conditions in Etruria and was found satisfactory by the Etruscans, for it lasted throughout the period of their independence.

We know from Greek and Roman historians that there were twelve cities in Etruria, though no doubt the list differed as the cities rose or waned in power. These city-states were united by 9 their common language and religion and formed a loose federation (see Chapter 7), but each had its own individual character and customs which spread over the territory within its control, so that their boundaries may be broadly assessed though they are not precisely known. The dominance of the metropolis within each city-state is evident: occasionally it seems smaller centres were destroyed or abandoned in favour of the city, and sometimes a network of roads may be traced, radiating from the city to lesser centres within its territory.

Local geology often dictated the choice of sites for cities and towns. The broad coastal plain of southern Etruria offered no naturally defensible sites, but the flat-topped rock citadels cut by watercourses from the inland plateau were ideal for defence, and those of a suitable size and in strategic positions were often selected for settlement. The cemeteries always lay outside the inhabited area, either at the flanks of the citadel, on a summit nearby or cut into the rock-face of neighbouring cliffs. In contrast, among the more mountainous scenery of northern Etruria, the Etruscan cities and towns were frequently placed on the steep side or summit of lofty hills, with their tombs cut into the surrounding slopes.

Cerveteri (ancient Caere) was the southern-most coastal city of Etruria, and this position, together with the local mineral resources, accounts for the city's early wealth. It was set upon a low citadel and surrounded by a city wall: 10 excavation is beginning to expose some of the urban area but the cemeteries are the most imposing Etruscan remains. Tombs lie at the base of the cliffs around the city and on adjacent hills, but by far the best-excavated and preserved cemetery, or necropolis, is that of Banditaccia, a 11 hill lying to the north, where a few of the tombs have been found with their contents intact. A road led from the city across the intervening 12 valley and down the length of the hill, branching to left and right in lesser streets leading to the doors of tombs. Many of the tombs are partly built above ground, but most have chambers

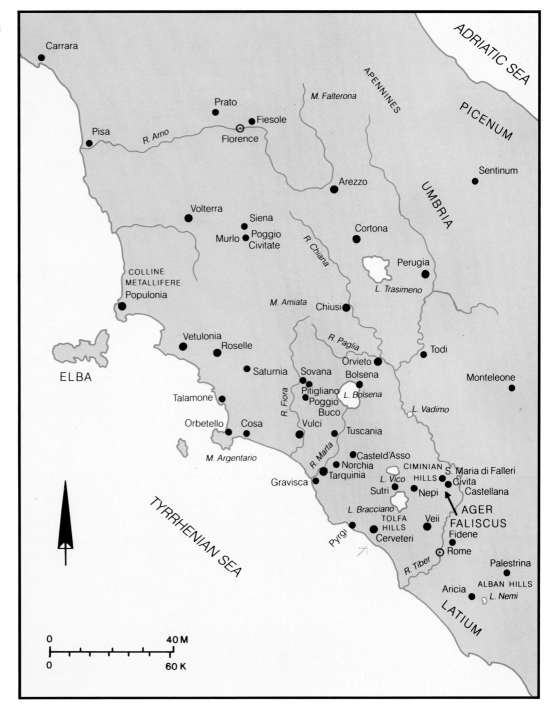

9 Map of ancient Etruria, showing the Etruscan cities and other major sites mentioned in the text.

ADRIATIC SEA

PICENUM

M. Falterona

APENNINES

Carrara

Prato

Fiesole

Florence

Pisa

R. Arno

UMBRIA

Arezzo

Sentinum

Volterra

Siena

Murlo • Poggio
Civitate

Cortona

R. Chiana

Perugia

COLLINE
METALLIFERE
Populonia

M. Amiata

Chiusi

L. Trasimeno

Vetulonia

Roselle

R. Paglia

Todi

ELBA

Saturnia

Sovana

Orvieto

Bolsena

Monteleone

Talamone

R. Fiora

Pitigliano

Poggio
Buco

L. Bolsena

L. Vadimo

Orbetello

Cosa

Vulci

Tuscania

M. Argentario

R. Marta

Casteld'Asso

CIMINIAN

S. Maria di Falleri

Norchia

HILLS

Civita

Graviska

Tarquinia

L. Vico

Sutri

Nepi

Castellana

TYRRHENIAN SEA

L. Bracciano

TOLFA
HILLS

Veii

AGER
FALISCUS

Fidene

Pyrgi

Cerveteri

Rome

Palestrina

R. Tiber

ALBAN HILLS

Aricia

L. Nemi

LATIUM

0   40 M

0   60 K

10 Drawing by S. J. Ainsley (1806–74) of the site of Cerveteri from the west. The Etruscan city was set on a plateau rising from the coastal plain, and was surrounded by low cliffs. The valleys of streams bound the plateau to the north and south, and the great cemeteries lie on the neighbouring flat-topped summits.

17 hewn from the rock, some carved to resemble the interiors of houses.

The exteriors of the tombs were constructed in various manners down the centuries. There are the early round mounds or tumuli, with a moulded base cut from the rock and topped with a heap of earth large enough to cover several tombs; smaller mounds with a single tomb; rows of tombs built in rectilinear terraces, and the later chambers cut deep into the rock with only their entrance at ground level.

From Cerveteri, a road ran down to the coast at Pyrgi (modern Santa Severa), one of the city's principal ports, famous in antiquity for its sanctuary. Over the last decades, the foundations of two temples and neighbouring buildings have been excavated here. The finds included fine temple terracottas, notably the plaque which covered the end of the central roof beam of Temple A, and three gold plaques, two inscribed in Etruscan and the third with a similar text in Phoenician/Punic script.

To the north of Cerveteri lay Tarquinia, while to the south and west of her territory was that of Veii, the early rival of Rome, which lay only eighteen kilometres to the south. Though sacked by the Romans in 396 BC, the site continued to be occupied in Roman times but was later deserted

and is now farmland. Both the acropolis and the city were girt by cliffs and walls; under the cliffs on the southern side was the Portonaccio sanctuary. Here a complex building has been excavated, including temple foundations, an altar and tanks, no doubt connected with the healing powers of the water; beautiful temple terracottas were brought to light, including statues which once adorned the roof of the temple. A great tunnel, the Ponte Sodo, was cut across the northern flank of the citadel to divert the flood waters of a neighbouring stream. To the west of the city is a rock-cut tunnel, or *cuniculus*, designed to carry water from one valley to another, a feat of engineering quite common in this region of Etruria. The Etruscan cemeteries of Veii are not well known but the tombs include two early painted chambers.

Inland of Veii and bounded by the right bank of the Tiber was the Ager Faliscus, the land of the Faliscans, who spoke a language akin to Latin but accepted much Etruscan culture. Their principal city was at Civita Castellana (ancient Falerii Veteres), a citadel nearly surrounded by towering cliffs. After the inhabitants were forced by the Romans to abandon this in 241 BC, they settled at Santa Maria di Falleri (ancient Falerii Novi), a site in open country nearby, where the fine city wall with turrets and gateways survives. To the north of Veii lay the two towns of Nepi and Sutri, called 'the gates of Etruria' by the Romans during the fourth century BC, since to the north and beyond the Ciminian Hills lay the territory of Tarquinia.

The city of Tarquinia was set upon a low summit where the coastal plain met the uplands in the valley of the Marta. The site now lies open, and survey and excavation have revealed areas of Etruscan and Roman streets and the foundations of a temple, now called the Ara della Regina, the pediment of which was graced with terracotta winged horses, now exhibited in Tarquinia Archaeological Museum. The modern town lies on the northern end of the neighbouring hill of Monterozzi, which in Etruscan times was covered by a huge cemetery and is now famed for its underground tombs, hewn from the rock and many with painted walls. Recent exploration of Gravisca (modern Porto Clementino), one of the ports of Tarquinia, has revealed evidence of the Greek merchants who resided there. A number of inland towns are known in the territory of Tarquinia; these include Tuscania, Norchia and Castel d'Asso.

13

The territory of Tarquinia extended up the valley of the Marta to the lake of Bolsena. Overlooking the northern shore of this lake was an Etruscan town with a fine defensive wall. To the east lay Orvieto (ancient Volsinii), set on a magnificent citadel of rock, surrounded by cliffs contents page and commanding the valleys of the Paglia and Chiana a little to the north of their junction with the Tiber. Though this rich city was sacked by the Romans in 264 BC, when its inhabitants were moved to a less defensible site, it was reoccupied during the medieval period and has remained a thriving centre. As a result, few Etruscan remains are known within the urban area, apart from the temple foundations in the Belvedere 18 Park. Etruscan cemeteries have been excavated below the cliffs: much of the Crocifisso del Tufo necropolis had been covered with fallen debris,

11 Aerial view of the Banditaccia cemetery, Cerveteri.

but excavation has revealed straight streets of small tombs built of stone, many with the name of the dead inscribed on the lintel above the entrance. Other tombs are scattered over the surrounding countryside, including two cut from the rock and with painted walls, often called the Golini tombs after their finder.

To the north of Tarquinia and west of lake Bolsena lay the territory of Vulci. The city itself was some eleven kilometres from the coast and set upon a low summit, whose steep scarps were bordered by the river Fiora and a tributary stream. The site was still occupied in Roman times but subsequently deserted; the whole district continued to be subject to malaria into this century. Recent excavation has exposed the well-built foundations of an Etruscan temple and Roman houses, but Vulci is chiefly renowned for its great bridge, the Ponte della Badia, whose arch is Roman in date but was perhaps raised from Etruscan foundations, and its rich cemeteries. Among the famous tombs at Vulci are the great tumulus called Cuccumella, approached by a long sloping entrance passage leading into a maze of underground tunnels, the 'Isis Tomb' in the Polledrara cemetery, and the François Tomb, which was cut into the cliff above the River Fiora and had painted chambers.

The large territory of Vulci included the coastal site of Cosa (modern Ansedonia), where a Latin colony was settled in 273 BC and surrounded by a wall of polygonal masonry, Orbetello, set on the strand linking Monte Argentario with the mainland, and Talamone, a rocky hill rising from the sea, where the site of an Etruscan temple has been found. Inland, the territory extended up to Monte Amiata; Etruscan towns are known at Poggio Buco, Pitigliano, Saturnia and Sovana (ancient Suana), where a deep rock-cut road leads down to a ravine with many tombs, some with elaborate façades.

The more mountainous landscape of northern Etruria begins to the north of the territory of Vulci, and the city of Roselle (ancient Rusellae) was set upon the shoulders and summit of a rounded hill and surrounded by a great wall of huge boulders. Though now somewhat inland, both Roselle and its neighbour Vetulonia prob-

56

12 LEFT Road cut deep in the rock, leading from Cerveteri to the Banditaccia cemetery. The surface is deeply worn by the wheels of carriages in Etruscan funerary processions.

13 RIGHT Drawing by S. J. Ainsley (1806–74) of Castel d'Asso and some neighbouring rock-cut tombs. The Etruscan town occupied the natural citadel in the middle distance. The tombs line the cliffs of the adjacent valleys and are mainly of the so-called dado type, with heavy mouldings at the top and false doors. The chambers are hewn from the rock below these façades and were entered by narrow passages.

ably once had access to the sea from a lagoon or bay, which has now silted up to form part of the coastal plain. To the north of this plain, Vetulonia crowns the summit of a steep-sided hill. Here, the principal Etruscan remains are the early tombs, some consisting of graves set within stone circles and others of chambers constructed with a square ground-plan rising to false domes. There are also traces of the Etruscan city wall, and a Roman street with adjacent houses has been excavated.

The territory of Roselle must have extended inland to border upon that of Chiusi (ancient Clusium), while to the north of Vetulonia lay Populonia, the only Etruscan city set directly upon the coast. This city, protected by outlying walls, is poised on a summit rising from the sea and overlooks a bay to the north with a long beach. Its cemeteries are on the low-lying land beside this bay and include finely constructed mounds and small built chambers. The territory of Populonia was rich in metal-bearing ores, particularly the iron ores of Elba, and the early cemeteries are covered by deep layers of iron slag, the waste from ores smelted in antiquity.

The city of Volterra (ancient Volaterrae) dominated north-west Etruria. Again, the metropolis was set upon a lofty summit, visible over a wide area and surrounded by a formidable fourth-century city wall, over six kilometres in length and built of large, squared blocks set in courses, which in some places still rise over five metres in height. Two Etruscan gateways survive. The urban area has been continuously occupied through Roman to modern times, but great landslides have carried away part of the hill-top, perhaps once honeycombed with tombs cut into the rock. Outside the city, chamber tombs of great families are known, usually roughly hewn from the rock, leaving a supporting central pillar. The few scattered Etruscan tombs known within the territory of Volterra suggest widespread farming settlements.

In the valley of the Arno, Pisa, once a port, was occupied in Etruscan times and Fiesole (ancient Faesulae), set upon a hill overlooking Florence from the north, was founded by the Etruscans and surrounded by a defensive wall.

14 The site of Volterra (*top*), set upon an imposing hill-top, dominates the surrounding countryside. (*Below*) The Grotta dei Marmini, an underground chamber tomb outside the walls of Volterra. Such family tombs served their owners over several generations. The urns, most with figures reclining on the lids, date from the 3rd to the 1st century BC. Drawings by S.J. Ainsley (1806–74).

Set in the hills to the south of Siena lies the rural site of Poggio Civitate, near Murlo, where recent excavation has revealed a complex of buildings with extraordinary terracotta architectural decorations dating to the seventh and sixth centuries BC. Towards the end of the latter century the site was destroyed, probably by the growing power of Chiusi.

The four cities of north-eastern Etruria, Chiusi, Arezzo, Cortona and Perugia, have all been occupied to this day, their continuing prosperity based upon the rich local agriculture. Chiusi lies in the fertile valley of the Chiana, which links the valley of the Tiber with that of the upper Arno, an ever-important route of communication, and the city was the first in this area to rise to prominence. Few traces of the Etruscans survive within the urban area, but interesting tombs, some with painted walls, lie among the adjacent farmlands. These tombs include the Poggio Gaiella, a natural hill-top with passages and tombs cut into the rock, and the so-called Tomb of the Grand Duke, which is entered through stone doors which swing open upon pivots and has a fine barrel vault.

Chiusi had a central position within a large territory which reached south to border upon that of Orvieto and west towards Roselle, and which to the north-east abutted upon the territories of Arezzo, Cortona and Perugia, each of which probably extended east into the valley of the upper Tiber. These three cities are set upon the summits or steep sides of bold hills, which rise above the farmland in the valleys surrounding Lake Trasimeno; medieval and modern building obscures most traces of the Etruscans within the urban areas, but a fine altar survives at Arezzo (ancient Arretium) and the city walls of Cortona and Perugia (ancient Perusia) include much Etruscan work. Outstanding tombs outside Cortona are the 'Melon of Camuscia', a large mound covering stone-built chambers, and the 'Cave of Pythagoras'. At the foot of the steep hill of Perugia lies the tomb of the Volumnii family, which was hewn from the rock and carved to resemble the architectural detail of the interior of a house.

In this sketch of the cities of Etruria, roads, bridges and city walls have been briefly men-

15 The Porta dell'Arco at Volterra. Three carved heads adorn the stones of the arch. Set in the 4th-century BC city wall, the present form of this gateway is probably a reconstruction of the 2nd or 1st century BC.

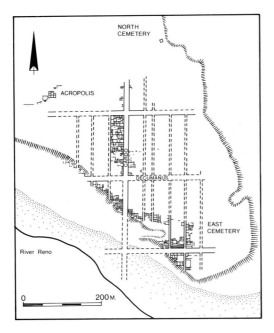

16 Plan of the Etruscan town at Marzabotto, near Bologna. The streets were laid out at right angles and oriented on the cardinal points of the compass. One broad main street ran north and south (*cardo*) and was intersected by three streets running east and west (*decumani*). Minor streets divided the blocks, in which the houses and working areas followed individual plans. An area of sacred buildings was set upon a neighbouring hill and the cemeteries lay outside the town.

tioned. Roads are chiefly known in the south of Etruria, where they were often cut through the soft rock with a drainage channel provided at either side. The earlier bridges were constructed of wooden beams supported by stone foundations, while arched bridges of stone were introduced in the later centuries BC. The first known fortifications of Etruscan sites were earthen banks with external ditches. The earliest city wall of stone, that at Roselle, constructed of uncut blocks, is dated to the sixth century BC. In the subsequent centuries many fine defensive walls were built of squared blocks set in regular courses; it seems they were often constructed as the dangers of the time required. The city wall of Veii is dated within the fifth century BC, while the great wall at Volterra may be from the following century. Polygonal masonry as found at Cosa was introduced to Etruria by the Romans. Arched gateways and turreted walls also belong to the last three centuries BC.

Few Etruscan urban centres have been fully explored, but present evidence suggests that the older cities, which had grown from earlier settlements, often had a haphazard arrangement, as many modern cities with medieval origins have today. It is clear, however, that by the sixth century BC the Etruscans were familiar with organised grid planning and practised it when building new cemeteries like those at Cerveteri or Orvieto and at new colonial sites in Campania and in the lower Po Valley. These include the port of Spina, which had a grid of canals serving as streets, and Marzabotto, a colony founded in the sixth century BC on a main route across the Apennines leading to Bologna (Etruscan Felsina). Much of this site has been excavated: sacred buildings on a neighbouring hill, or acropolis, included temples and a platform from which auspices were taken, all carefully oriented to face due south. Cemeteries of small tombs built of slabs lie outside the inhabited area. Here the streets were aligned on the cardinal points of the compass; they had cobbled pavements and deep drainage ditches, covered with stone slabs. The houses within this strict grid plan show many variations, but often a long corridor led from the street into a courtyard, which was surrounded by rooms. These houses had foundations of river stones, walls which must have been of unfired brick, and tiled roofs. Many houses had wells in the courtyard and terracotta water-pipes were found; dwellings and workshops mingled in the habitation area.

More research is needed before the development of the house in Etruria is fully understood. Huts of the Villanovan period have already been described; such huts continued in use during the seventh century BC, as has been shown by excavation and by the replica of the interior of a hut cut into the rock under a great tumulus in the Banditaccia cemetery at Cerveteri. However, research has now demonstrated that rectangular houses with stone foundations, unfired brick walls and tiled roofs were adopted in Etruria during the seventh century and had become common by the sixth; a striking example is the buildings of Poggio Civitate, mentioned above. There can be no doubt that this new technique of building was inspired by the Greeks, but the Etruscans used it in their own manner and with a heavy emphasis upon the terracotta decorations of the roof, which recall the Italian tradition of wooden embellishments to roofs.

It is unlikely that the ground-plan of Etruscan houses was uniform in rural and urban environments, or during all the centuries of their development. Nevertheless, the tombs show a recurring arrangement of an entrance passage with rooms on either side, a central hall and three parallel rooms beyond, a plan already familiar by the sixth century BC. It is clear that heavy wooden beams were used in Etruscan houses, as they were in temples; this is shown in their tombs cut from the rock, which have many details of roofing, doors and windows. Vitruvius 17 (*On Architecture*, VI, 3, 1) has left us a description of later halls, or *atria*, in Etruscan houses; these had a central opening to the sky to give light, and heavy beams set into the walls supported a roof designed to shed rainwater into a pool beneath.

The domestic architecture of the Etruscans was influenced by the building techniques and design of the Greeks and was akin to that of the early Romans, and this is also true of their temples. At first, the gods were worshipped in open-air sanctuaries but at least by the beginning of the sixth century BC, as the gods came to be seen in anthropomorphic form, temples were built and images of the gods placed inside, while most ceremonies were performed at altars set outside the buildings.

The Etruscans continued to use wood in the construction of their temples long after this practice was generally abandoned by the Greeks; no doubt this was partly due to the lack of fine building stone in Etruria and to the local availability of hardwood trees in her forests. Though stone was sometimes used for the walls or other parts of the structure of temples, more often it was only used for the foundations, and the walls were built of unfired brick covered with plaster, with columns and beams of wood, protected where necessary by decorative terracotta revetment plaques. Since the elements of unfired brick and wood have disappeared in the course of time, only the stone foundations and terracotta embellishments are left as evidence of Etruscan 18 temples.

Temples with a single room, or *cella*, which housed the image of the god, are known in Etruria, but the principal form of Etruscan

17 Tomb of the Capitals, Cerveteri. The chambers are cut from the rock to resemble the interior of a house, with an entrance passage flanked by a room on either side, a central hall and three rooms beyond. Two columns support the 'beams' and 'joists' in the hall, and above there appears to be thatching. The tomb dates to the early 6th century BC.

temple had three *cellae* at the back, a ground plan which recalls that of their domestic architecture and which was also well established by the end of the sixth century BC. We may turn to Vitruvius again for the description of an ideal Etruscan temple. He writes (*On Architecture*, IV, 7, and III, 3, 5) that a temple built in the Etruscan manner should be almost square, but slightly longer than wide, and that the front half should be filled with two rows of four columns, placed in line with the walls of three *cellae* which should complete the rear half of the temple, providing a setting for the images of a triad of gods. The general accuracy of this account is confirmed by the surviving foundations of Etruscan temples. These foundations also demonstrate that, unlike the Greeks but in common with the Romans, the Etruscans often designed their temples to be approached by steps from the front only, with a blank wall at the back.

Vitruvius noted that the elevation of Tuscan temples, with their great wooden beams, had a top-heavy appearance, and this must have been emphasised by the terracotta embellishments which were set on the roof and covered the beams. The Etruscans often placed terracotta sculpture and other decorations above the gable and ridge of the roof of their temples (*acroteria*); this tradition appears to have sprung, not from the inspiration of Greek architecture, but from the old Italian practice of adorning the roofs of dwellings. The exposed lengths of the wooden beams were protected by terracotta revetment plaques, often moulded with repeating patterns. Unlike the Greeks, the Etruscans in early times left open the triangular space beneath the gable, though they covered the ends of the major roof beams with terracotta plaques, sometimes modelled in relief, like that from Pyrgi mentioned below. In the final centuries BC, the Etruscans did fill this space, or pediment, with sculpture, often composed in complicated groups. The roof was tiled, and along the eaves, masking the junctions of the rows of tiles, was set a line of decorative antefixes, moulded in many differing forms. All these terracotta decorations would have been painted in bright colours, so Etruscan temples must have had a very striking appearance.

18 The stone foundations, or *podium*, of the Etruscan temple in the Belvedere Park, Orvieto. Little survives of most Etruscan temples except the stone foundations and terracotta decorations. The columns and beams of wood and the walls of unfired brick have disappeared.

19 Model of an Etruscan temple as described by Vitruvius. (Università di Roma 'La Sapienza'.)

3 The Orientalising Period 700–600 BC

20 Gold brooch (*fibula*) with a small bow formed of three curving tubes and a long catch-plate of gold sheet. Ten pairs of free-standing lions, all glancing back over their shoulder, are set upon the catch-plate, while further lions, sphinxes and the heads of lions and horses decorate the bow and the tip and butt of the catch-plate. Details are picked out in small gold globules (granulation). From Vulci, 675–650 BC. L. 18.6 cm.

Surviving inscriptions show that the people of ancient Etruria learnt to write early in the seventh century BC, adopting the alphabet used by the Greeks of Cuma (Cumae), a daughter colony of the Euboean settlement on Ischia founded on the coast of Italy just to the north of Naples. Since the inhabitants of seventh-century Etruria wrote in the Etruscan language, it is certain that the Etruscans were established there by that time and we may confidently call them by this name.

From the seventh to the first century BC, the seven centuries of their individual artistic expression, the Etruscans were closely in touch with many of their Mediterranean neighbours and contemporaries and were often inspired by foreign examples, principally those of the Greeks. Though they were never mere peripheral imitators, the Etruscans did follow the major styles of the Greeks, so that it is customary to call the artistic periods of Etruria by the same names as those of Greece, that is, the Orientalising period, followed by the Archaic, Classical and Hellenistic periods. In Greece, these styles had an organic growth, arising from contemporary historic and intellectual developments. This background was alien to the Etruscans, who at times appear to have accepted the outward forms without assimilating the inner content. Yet it may be said that of all the contemporary neighbours of the Greeks, the Etruscans proved themselves most

sensitive to the beauty of Greek visual art, and their craftsmanship, particularly in their metal-work, often rivalled that of the Greeks. Though they used Greek art forms, styles and motifs, the Etruscans were always selective in adapting them to their own conventions and to express Etruscan taste, sometimes that of a single city-state.

Though the Etruscans learnt to write in the seventh century BC and in later centuries probably used their literacy to write books of history, among other forms of literature, almost none of these texts have come down to us (see Chapter 7). The Etruscan language had become little used by the first century BC and was obsolete by the early centuries AD, so unlike the books written in Greek or Latin, which were copied and recopied during medieval times, Etruscan texts written on perishable material have disappeared. Thus, in piecing together the history of the Etruscans, we have to rely upon archaeological evidence and on references made by Greek and Roman authors, who were usually describing the events of their own history and seldom mention the internal affairs of Etruria. Moreover, Greek and Roman historians often wrote in the critical spirit of rivalry and long after the events they describe, frequently dealing with centuries only just emerging from legendary times with few contemporary records to consult. Nevertheless, Roman historians were concerned to recount as much as possible of the early history of their city, and they were interested in Rome's debt to her Etruscan neighbours during the regal period of the seventh and sixth centuries BC.

In this way, an important story involving seventh-century Etruria has come down to us: Livy (I, 34) and Pliny (*Natural History*, XXXV, 152) mention that Demaratus, a nobleman of Corinth, fled from his native city during a political crisis in the middle of the seventh century BC and settled at Tarquinia, which he knew from previous trading contacts. One of his sons, called Lucumo by Roman historians, married a noble lady of Tarquinia, named Tanaquil. Since they could not advance themselves at Tarquinia because Lucumo was not of pure Etruscan lineage, the couple set out for Rome, and Livy tells us that when they reached the

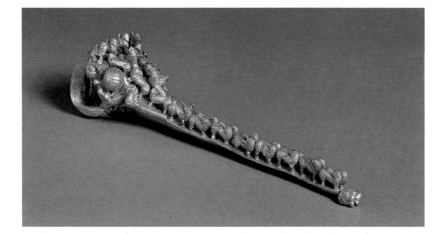

Janiculum in their wagon an eagle plucked Lucumo's cap from his head, then rose in the sky and descended to replace it again. Tanaquil, 'a woman skilled in celestial prodigies, as was the case with most Etruscans', joyfully interpreted the omen, telling Lucumo to expect greatness, and her prophecy was fulfilled when he became king of Rome as Lucius Tarquinius the Elder.

Demaratus is said to have brought Greek craftsmen with him to Etruria and, whatever the truth behind this account, it is certain that many new ideas reached Etruria during the seventh century BC, as did a great number of imported goods. Such stimuli from Greece and the east Mediterranean drew Etruria out of the European sphere, to which she had been indebted since Italian Late Bronze Age times, and turned her attention towards the Mediterranean world. The local architecture was transformed, together with other major and minor arts and many political and social styles of life in Etruria. The rural communities of former centuries were developing into larger units: the extraordinary complex of buildings at Poggio Civitate has been explained not only as the residence of a priestly king but also as an important assembly place of northern Etruria. Above all, in the course of the seventh century, the political structure of city-states was firmly established in Etruria, with the attendant emphasis upon the chief city or metropolis within each city-state, and an aristocratic social organisation. Both these institutions were to last until the end of Etruscan independence. It should be added here that during the Orientalising period inhumation, or burial of the dead, became the most common funerary rite at several southern cities, while in the north of

21 Objects said to be from the 'Isis Tomb' in the Polledrara cemetery at Vulci:

a (*top left*) Ostrich egg carved in very low relief and used as a vessel. Probably carved in Etruria by an artist from the east Mediterranean who was familiar with Corinthian vase-painting, *c.*625–600 BC. H. 16.2 cm.

b (*bottom left*) Faience flask with a hieroglyphic inscription expressing New Year greetings. Probably made at Naucratis, Egypt, *c.*625–550 BC. H. 13 cm.

c (*right*) Gypsum perfume-bottle (*alabastron*). Perhaps made in a Greek city of Asia Minor, *c.*600 BC. H. 45 cm.

Etruria cremation continued to be practised.

The incoming influences had a great impact upon the southern and coastal areas of Etruria, which were both open to trade by sea and rich in metal ores, whose exploitation must account for the great purchasing power exhibited by the Etruscans at this time. However, it is becoming increasingly clear that the inland cities of northern Etruria did not lag far behind. The vast new wealth is demonstrated by the tombs of aristocratic families, who must have been able to assert their princely position, control the sources of wealth and benefit from the ensuing trade and other exchange systems. Some of these tombs have been mentioned above, like the great seventh-century tumuli of Cerveteri.

Especially rich tombs appear at several sites in Etruria, including Vetulonia, Tarquinia and Cerveteri, where the Regolini-Galassi Tomb was found intact: its contents are now exhibited in the Vatican Museums. At Palestrina (ancient Praeneste) in Latium, the Barberini and Bernadini Tombs were found undisturbed; their goods are now displayed among the great Etruscan collection of the Villa Giulia Museum in Rome.

At this time, luxury goods reached Etruria from Egypt, the Phoenician cities of the Levant, north Syria and Assyria, Cyprus, Asia Minor and Greece. During this period, Greek art was under the influence of the high cultures of the east Mediterranean area and some of these imports were in the resulting Greek Orientalising style. Etruscan craftsmen borrowed from all these sources, mingling motifs, copying imported objects in different materials and adapting incoming elements to Italian traditions, so that they created a thoroughly eclectic Orientalising style of their own.

22b Tridacna shells from the Indian Ocean or Red Sea were carved in the east Mediterranean area and imported to Etruria. Ostrich eggs came from Mesopotamia or Africa: some were already dec-
21a orated but others were worked in Etruria by foreign artists. Faïence objects from Egypt included beads, scarabs and other trinkets, as well
21b as vessels. Ivory was introduced, some pieces carved in north Syria or the Phoenician cities but others in Etruria, perhaps by craftsmen from

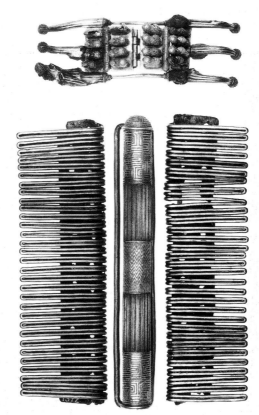

23 LEFT

a (*top*) Gold-plated silver clasp or 'bolt-*fibula*', decorated with free-standing sphinxes, with details in granulation. From the Tomb of the Five Chairs, Cerveteri, *c.*675–650 BC. L. 9.1 cm.

b (*bottom*) Gold, silver and bronze clasp or 'comb-*fibula*'. The two outer elements, each with a row of hooks along one side, would be sewn to the opposite edges of a garment and united by attaching both to the bars on the central tube. Such clasps were used to fasten a mantle at the shoulder (see Fig. 30). About 675–650 BC. L. 12.4 cm.

22 LEFT

a (*left*) Gold perfume-bottle (*alabastron*) with double lines of granulation in a guilloche band on the neck and rows of zigzags covering the body. Said to be from Palestrina, Latium, *c*.650–600 BC. H. 15.2 cm.

b (*right*) Tridacna shell carved with a human head and with incised decoration representing two winged sphinxes, lotus buds and flowers. Tridacna shells come from the Indian Ocean and Red Sea. This one was carved in the east Mediterranean area and imported into Etruria. It probably served as a container for cosmetics. Probably from Vulci, 700–650 BC. W. 21.8 cm.

24 RIGHT Pair of gold bracelets, decorated with granulation and repeating figured patterns embossed by the use of stamps from the back. One set of panels shows three women, each grasping in either hand a tree-like plant terminating in a palmette. The second set of panels, at either end of each bracelet, depicts a 'Master of Animals' flanked by lions. Both themes derive from Phoenician motifs. From the Galeassi Tomb, Palestrina, Latium, *c*.675–650 BC. L. 18.5 and 18.6 cm.

these areas, fleeing from the expanding power of the Assyrians. Carved objects of fine stone also reached Etruria, some perhaps from the Greek cities of Asia Minor. Silver and silver-gilt vessels from the Phoenician cities or Cyprus were imported and these and other prototypes were copied in gold and silver, so that Etruscan gold cups or bowls became famous among the Greeks. A beautiful example covered in delicate designs in granulation is now in the Victoria and Albert Museum in London.

The Etruscan élite of the Orientalising period clearly delighted in the display of luxury objects and this is fully reflected in their jewellery. Some forms and decorative motifs were borrowed from abroad, largely from the Phoenicians, but local traditions were also maintained, particularly in the case of brooches (*fibulae*), but with an entirely new splendour. Among all the Etruscan craftsmen, it was perhaps the goldsmiths who responded most vigorously to the new wealth of their patrons, creating not only brooches but also clasps for fastening mantles, earrings, bracelets, hair-rings and other jewellery of great beauty and technical skill, employing delicate granulation, filigree and embossing.

The Italian tradition of burnished black/brown pottery continued, but quite early during the seventh century true bucchero was developed. This is a distinctive black lustrous ware, made of a purified clay, turned on a potter's wheel and burnished before firing in a kiln with a restricted supply of oxygen, so that the iron oxides in the clay turned black. Early bucchero, beginning in about 675 BC, was of extremely fine quality with thin walls and elegant shapes, which sometimes followed older Italian traditions but at other times imitated Greek, often Corinthian, pottery prototypes. Sharing the eclectic tendencies of Etruscan craftsmen during this period, the potters often modelled their vessels upon metalwork and luxury materials and included motifs of animals and humans, a trend which became common during the second half of the century.

Greek painted pottery continued to be imported and imitated in Etruria. At first the potters were influenced by the Euboean Greeks of Pithekoussai and Cuma. As the century pro-

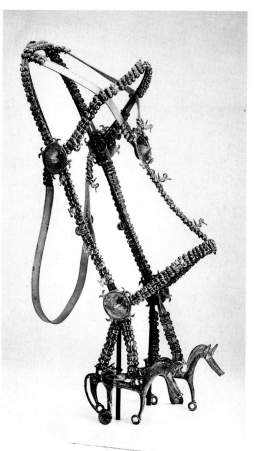

26 LEFT Bronze horse-bit and ornaments from a bridle. The cheek-pieces of the snaffle bit are cast in the form of horses, a motif perhaps inspired by models from the Near East. Other elements follow European bronzework traditions. The bridle is one of a pair and was probably made in northern Etruria, 700–650 BC. H. on modern frame 56 cm.

25 LEFT Bucchero pottery of the 7th century BC with incised decoration and dotted fans. *From left to right*:

a Jar with two handles. The shape is Italian. 675–625 BC. H. 20.25 cm.

b Cup (*kotyle*), its shape derived from Corinthian prototypes. 675–625 BC. H. 9.9 cm.

c Jug (*olpe*) also derived from Corinthian prototypes (see Fig. 27d). 650–600 BC. H. 15 cm.

d Chalice supported by moulded openwork struts and female figures holding strands of their hair in both hands. The design was perhaps inspired by east Mediterranean models. From Chiusi or Volterra, *c*.630–600 BC. H. 19.5 cm.

gressed, more pottery was imported from Corinth and this became the principal source of inspiration among the potters of Etruria, who strove to reproduce its fabric and motifs. Several shapes of this Corinthian pottery and its Etruscan imitations emphasise an interest in, and probably the importation of, perfume and wine.

Imported bronze objects of the seventh century BC and their Etruscan imitations also demonstrate a very wide-ranging trade and suggest the introduction of new social customs, such as the drinking of wine, among aristocratic families. Already during the eighth century, bronze objects made in Etruria show influence from central Europe and the east Mediterranean area. The following century saw a crescendo of bronze imports to Italy from the east, including Assyria, Urartu and Phrygia, and these had a profound effect upon the work of Etruscan bronzesmiths. The fine bronze embellishments for a pair of

horse bridles, for instance, show motifs perhaps 26 inspired from as far away as Iran and central Europe. The bridles may have been intended for the horses of a cart or chariot, perhaps used on ceremonial occasions. Tools and arms were now principally made of iron but most armour continued to be made of bronze. Gradually the Etruscans abandoned the helmets and shields of the type used during the Villanovan period and adopted the Corinthian helmet, the large 87 bronze shield of Greek infantrymen (hoplites) and greaves. It has been suggested that the bronze discs worn by warriors to protect their heart (*kardiophylakes*) were inspired by Assyrian 28 armour, yet some Etruscan examples are decorated in traditional Italian style. Other personal equipment of this time shows contacts far to the east; an example is a pair of belt-clasps of bronze 29a with iron inlay, whose technique and design may find parallels in the Caucasian region.

27 Etruscan painted pottery of the 7th century BC. *From left to right*:

a Jar (*olla*) with two handles, the shoulder decorated with birds. Attributed to the 'Heron Class' and made in southern Etruria, probably at Cerveteri. The decoration follows Greek prototypes. 700–650 BC. H. 20.3 cm.

b Perfume-bottle (*aryballos*), the shoulder decorated with a band of dogs. Made in southern Etruria. From Viterbo, *c*.650–625 BC. H. 13 cm.

c Perfume-bottle (*aryballos*) decorated with incised scales. Made in southern Etruria, 650–600 BC. H. 9 cm.

d Jug (*olpe*) decorated with two bands of incised and overlapping semicircles. Like **c**, the shape and decoration derive from Corinthian prototypes. About 600 BC. H. 20 cm.

Among the outstanding household bronzes both imported and copied in Etruria at this time are tripod-stands and embossed bronze supports for bowls, which were often embellished with the heads of griffins or other creatures at the rim and with human-headed sirens as handle attachments. Prototypes of this exotic form of bowl are known from Urartu, as well as related types from Assyria, Phrygia, Cyprus and Greece. Terracotta and bronze replicas survive of a traditional

31 Italian type of chair, based upon basketwork models, but other bronzes hint at the introduction to Etruria of new forms of wooden furniture,

29b including chairs and beds. These fragmentary remains of fine objects may serve to remind us of the host of perishable materials, particularly woven fabrics and wood, which have not come down to us but must have played an important part in ancient trade.

The wide-ranging trade of the seventh century BC was accompanied by the arrival of many innovations which transformed life in Etruria. It was a crucial century for the Etruscans, when traditions were established which were to last until the end of their independent civilisation. Not least among these was the custom of painting the walls of some of their tombs. It is not yet

clear what inspired this large-scale painting, though motifs were borrowed freely from the decoration of pottery; it may be that already during the seventh century the plaster surfaces of the unfired brick walls of their buildings were painted and that the painted decoration of the walls of their tombs reflects this custom. At any rate, the earliest known tomb with wall-paintings, the Tomb of the Ducks at Veii, is now believed to date to the first half of the seventh century, and this was followed by other painted tombs at Veii and Cerveteri in a later Orientalising style.

Large-scale sculpture had a more hesitant beginning in Etruria. The people of the Villanovan period had modelled small figures in terracotta and cast others in bronze, and some entirely indigenous artistic forms, like the so-

31 called Canopic urns of Chiusi, have claims to be termed sculpture. In other cases, small imported objects with modelled human or animal forms were copied on a larger scale. During the seventh century there also appear in tombs stone statues and some of terracotta, like those from the Tomb of the Five Chairs at Cerveteri, which seem to 30 follow north Syrian or other east Mediterranean prototypes.

28 LEFT Decorated bronze disc worn as armour to protect the heart. Such discs were probably inspired by prototypes from the east Mediterranean area. They are found inland in Etruria and in east central Italy. 675–625 BC. D. 22 cm.

29 BELOW

a (*top*) Cast bronze belt-clasp with iron inlay. The animal motifs and metalwork technique may have been inspired by prototypes from the Near East. About 650–600 BC. L. together 21.5 cm.

b (*bottom*) Bronze plaque with repoussé decoration. Such plaques may have adorned wooden furniture, a vehicle or perhaps the door of a house. The style suggests both east Mediterranean and Corinthian inspiration. 650–600 BC. L. 35.5 cm.

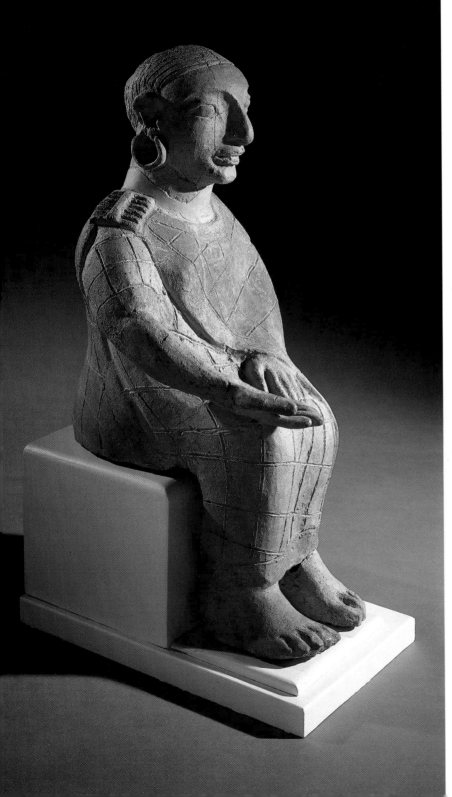

30 LEFT Terracotta seated figure wearing a chequered tunic and mantle, fastened with a clasp at the shoulder (see Fig. 23b). The figure has been restored with a female head, but the body is probably that of a man. The statue was found in a side-chamber of a tomb, with other similar figures which were once enthroned in five chairs carved from the rock. An altar in the chamber suggests that funerary rites were performed there in honour of ancestors, whom these figures may represent. From the Tomb of the Five Chairs, Cerveteri, c.625–600 BC. H. 54.5 cm.

31 ABOVE Terracotta cinerary urn, the lid modelled as a human head and the body set upon a model chair. Such urns, which are found in the neighbourhood of Chiusi, are known as 'Canopic', since they bear a superficial resemblance to the Canopic urns of Egypt. The holes piercing the head were probably used to attach a mask. From Chiusi, c.625–600 BC. H. 58 cm.

By 600 BC, the main features of Etruscan civilisation had been established and the aristocratic class might well have felt secure in the position of their cities in west central Italy. The following century was a time of confidence and expansion for the Etruscans. As we have seen, a nobleman from Tarquinia had become king of Rome under the name of Lucius Tarquinius the Elder, traditionally in 616 BC. Perhaps this brought the neutrality of Rome, for at about this time the Etruscans advanced southwards into Campania, probably using the inland route along the valleys of the Sacco and Liri. There they are said to have founded twelve cities, including Capua (modern Santa Maria di Capua Vetere) in the Campanian plain and bordering upon the territories of the Greek coastal colonies. This juxtaposition led to much artistic exchange between the Etruscans of Campania and the neighbouring Greeks during the next two centuries, but was also a potential source of rivalry.

During the sixth century BC, Etruscans from the northern cities crossed the Apennines and placed colonies in the lower Po Valley, establishing Etruscan culture in that region. They founded Marzabotto, settled at Bologna, which was already old, and created the Adriatic port of Spina. Advancing north of the Po, they certainly settled both at the port of Adria, which would have given them access to the valley of the Adige leading up to the Brenner Pass over the Alps, and in the area around Mantua, though it is not clear how far west they penetrated along the Po Valley. At this time, the Etruscans most closely achieved the description of Cato (quoted by Servius, *Commentary on Virgil's Aeneid* XI, 567): 'nearly all Italy had been under the domination of the Etruscans'.

No rivals to Etruscan power had yet emerged in the north, but they now faced the Greeks in Campania and soon a confrontation with Greeks also arose in the Tyrrhenian Sea. About 600 BC, Greeks from the city of Phocaea in Asia Minor had defeated the Carthaginians at sea and founded a colony at Massilia (modern Marseilles) at the mouth of the Rhone on the south coast of France. Some forty years later, they established a settlement at Alalia (modern Aleria) on the east

coast of Corsica, and this was enlarged by new colonists from Phocaea when all the Greek cities of Asia Minor were threatened by the Persians after the fall of Lydia in 546 BC. The Etruscans and Carthaginians were close allies at this time and alarm must have been felt both in the coastal cities of Etruria and by the Carthaginians, now assuming an imperial role among the Phoenician colonists of the west including those of Sardinia. About 535 BC, their combined fleets met the Phocaeans in battle off Alalia; the Phocaeans won a narrow victory but lost so many ships that they abandoned Corsica, where the Etruscans subsequently placed a colony.

In 524 BC, the Etruscans again met the Greeks in battle, this time on land and in Campania. Dionysius of Halicarnassus (VII, 3 and 4) tells us that the Etruscans attempted to take Cuma with an army of half a million men but were repulsed by a much smaller number of Greeks under the leadership of Aristodemos of Cuma, who killed the Etruscan general in battle. Shortly afterwards, the Etruscans suffered another serious reverse, when the last Etruscan king of Rome was expelled from the city and the Roman Republic was established, traditionally in 509 BC.

Many tales were told in later centuries concerning the Etruscan kings of Rome and their families. Dionysius of Halicarnassus (III, 61) relates how, after being defeated in battle, Etruscans brought Tarquinius the Elder their symbols of authority. Romans of the late Republic and Empire believed these were then adopted by the Roman state, including the *fasces*, or bundle of rods with an axe at the centre, which was carried by lictors before the Consuls. Tarquinius the Elder was credited with great building projects at Rome, including draining the Forum and beginning the temple of Jupiter on the Capitol. He was succeeded by his son-in-law, Servius Tullius, who was said to have initiated some democratising reforms, particularly in the army. He in turn was succeeded by Lucius Tarquinius the Proud, who is said to have enlarged Rome's prestige and leadership among her Latin neighbours and to have continued major building works in the city. However, the arrogance of the

32 Bronze bust of a woman, probably representing a goddess, holding a horned bird. The bust is made of hammered sheets of bronze, riveted together, while the hand and bird are cast. The bird was once covered with gold leaf. The figure wears a thin tunic, necklace and a belt, which is decorated with a maeander pattern. The base has a repoussé pattern of monsters derived from Corinthian vase painting, but the gesture of the left hand touching the breast was inspired by an east Mediterranean source. From the 'Isis Tomb', Polledrara cemetery, Vulci, 600–575 BC. H. 34 cm.

Tarquin family alienated both the aristocracy and people of Rome and led to the revolution which established the Republic. Livy (II, 9–14) recounts that Lars Porsenna, king of Clusium (modern Chiusi), subsequently beseiged Rome in order to win back the throne for the Tarquins but that he was unsuccessful. A little later we hear of an Etruscan defeat near Aricia in Latium. After this the Etruscans withdrew, tacitly acknowledging the rising power of Rome as leader of the Latin peoples and the loss of the inland route to Campania.

The internal history of Etruria during this period is obscure, though the archaeological record suggests the cities were very individualistic at this time and there may well have been rivalries between them. Smaller family tombs and the terraces or rows of modest chamber tombs of equal size at Cerveteri or Orvieto suggest the existence of a new middle class, some perhaps merchants. Etruria continued to attract imports on a large scale, the great majority coming from Greece, and immigrant craftsmen, some from the Greek cities of Asia Minor which were under pressure from the Persians. Above all, it was during the sixth century BC that the Etruscans abandoned their eclectic style of the previous Orientalising period and decisively turned to Greece for artistic inspiration. The century saw a rapid development in sculpture, painting and the minor arts in Etruria.

The rich 'Isis Tomb' at Vulci contained not only the imported luxury goods described above but also an extraordinary bust of a woman made **32** from thin sheets of bronze riveted together: this technique was used by contemporary Greeks and the bust shows a mingling of east Mediterranean and Greek motifs. A half life-size gypsum statue **back cover** of a woman from the same tomb was probably made by an indigenous craftsman at Vulci but undoubtedly follows Greek, perhaps Peloponnesian, models. Both these figures date to the first half of the sixth century. An urn from near **inside front cover** Chiusi in the form of a standing man was made during the middle of the century; the idea of placing the ashes of the dead in an urn of human form was already well established but now the style is clearly derived from Greece.

Like the earliest stone sculpture known from Etruria, which has been mentioned above, these statues were placed in tombs and, in strong contrast with Greek practice, the Etruscans generally restricted the use of stone for sculpture to funerary monuments. This may have been partly because of the lack of fine stone in parts of Etruria – the marble of Carrara was not discovered and exploited until the first century BC – but there also seems to have existed a traditional, perhaps religious, reluctance to carve in stone except for funerary use. During the Archaic period, stone sculptures, all associated with tombs, took several local forms. Outstanding among these are slabs carved in relief from Tarquinia, which seem to have been part of the architecture of tombs. At Vulci and in the surrounding area, fine statues carved in the round stood as guardians at the entrance of tombs. At Chiusi, tomb-markers (*cippi*) were sculpted, some with figures in the round and others carved in low relief, with scenes of everyday life, while in northern Etruria, notably at Vetulonia and Volterra, tombstones (*stelai*) were carved in relief with representations of the dead.

With stone usually reserved for use in funerary monuments, the sculpture of Etruria was largely of terracotta and bronze, both materials that require skills of modelling rather than of carving. Terracotta sculpture took many forms, among the most important of which were the embellishments of temples and houses, described above (Chapter 2). Down the centuries the styles of these decorations conformed with contemporary art and, as with other later Archaic sculpture in Etruria, influence may be discerned both from the Greek cities of Asia Minor and from Athens. A very high level of achievement was reached during the sixth century BC, with many charming series of antefixes, often of heads, sometimes enlarged with a surround in the form of a shell. There were also revetment plaques, now often decorated with scenes of gods and human figures at banquets, sports or other events. Outstanding examples of sculpture include those set on the roof of the building at Poggio Civitate, some executed in a two-

dimensional silhouette form while others are fully modelled in the round, and the four beautiful statues from Veii depicting the Greek myth of Apollo's contest with Herakles over the Ceryneian hind, or deer, sacred to Artemis. These adorned the ridge of the roof of the Portonaccio temple and are now in the Villa Giulia Museum at Rome. Though these statues show Athenian influence, the setting and conception of this group, so full of latent energy, seems entirely Etruscan. The group has been attributed to Vulca of Veii, the only Etruscan artist we know by name, and his school; Varro (quoted by Pliny, *Natural History*, XXXV, 157) recalled that Vulca was summoned to Rome during the regal period to model the terracotta statue of Jupiter for the Capitoline temple.

Splendid terracotta sarcophagi and cinerary urns were also made at this time, with the most outstanding series produced at Cerveteri. This series includes two famous sarcophagi, now in the Villa Giulia Museum and in the Louvre in Paris, with contented married couples shown reclining upon the lids, while the chests are modelled in the form of a bed or couch (*kline*).

Since bronze can be melted down for re-use, few large-scale bronze statues from Etruria have come down to us, but a great series of votive statuettes has survived. Both large statues and statuettes were dedicated to the gods at sanctuaries in anticipation of or gratitude for favours received by worshippers. Hollow-cast large-scale bronze sculpture appears in Etruria by the end of the Archaic era. A famous example is the Wolf of the Capitol, which, though found in Rome and now in the Capitoline Museums there, may have been made by a sculptor from Veii. Bronze votive statuettes appear during the sixth century BC and include representations of gods and goddesses, warriors, men and women, youths and maidens, some clearly depicting the dedicators. Many are of great beauty and technical skill, though their 34 poses tend to be rather stiff and motionless. The Etruscans also loved to adorn their bronze utensils with figures, and these too are often minor masterpieces.

The painting of the walls of tombs had begun at Veii and Cerveteri during the seventh century

BC. During the Archaic period this practice spread to Tarquinia, which became the major centre for this art throughout the subsequent centuries, though other cities, notably Chiusi, Orvieto and Vulci, also adopted the custom. The wall-paintings of Etruscan tombs are almost the only surviving sequence of large-scale painting from the classical world until the Romans began to paint the walls of their houses in the late Republican era, and they provide us with evidence for the progress of monumental painting from the Orientalising to the Hellenistic periods.

During the sixth century BC, large-scale paintings were occasionally applied to terracotta slabs, some of which are known to have come from tombs though others may have adorned temples or houses. The Boccanera plaques come from a tomb in the Banditaccia cemetery at Cerveteri; the terracotta was covered in a light undercoat and then painted in red and black, the style reflecting that of Corinthian vase-painting. However, the paintings were usually achieved in fresco technique: the walls of tombs hewn from the rock were smoothed and covered with plaster (probably kept damp for some time by the moisture in the rock), the scene was quickly sketched in *graffito* or painted outlines, and then while the plaster was still wet, the paint was filled in. In this technique, the paint sinks into the plaster and as long as the plaster survives, so does the painting.

The style of Etruscan tomb paintings was always closely related to that of the contemporary painting of vases or the engraving on bronzes but the range of colours soon exceeded those possible in vase-painting, including variations of blues and greens. At first, the figures were always set in a single plane, the heads in profile, the shoulders often frontal and the legs again in profile, with the outlines filled in with flat colours and some added details. Early in the sixth century, Corinthian vase-painting provided most models for this large-scale art and later in the century influence from the Greek cities of Asia Minor becomes apparent but, by about the middle of the Archaic period, Athenian painted pottery was a major source of inspiration for the artists. Etruscan tomb paintings of the late sixth and early fifth centuries have many joyous scenes of out-of-doors life, of hunting or fishing, games or sports, as well as funerary games and convivial banquets. These paintings are a major source of information concerning Etruscan everyday life of the time.

Corinthian pottery continued to be imported and imitated in Etruria during the early Archaic period, particularly fine vases being made at Vulci. Delightful perfume-bottles followed models from both the Greek cities of Asia Minor and from

35 Five painted terracotta plaques, known as the Boccanera Plaques after the two brothers who found them in a small tomb in 1874. The slabs with sphinxes probably flanked the door, while the three with the figured scene covered the rear wall. The subject is the Judgement of Paris. On the left, Paris is approached by Hermes, followed by Athena, Hera and Aphrodite. To the right is a woman, probably Helen, with three attendants who carry perfume-bottles and a casket for toilet articles. From the Banditaccia cemetery, Cerveteri, *c*.560–550 BC. H. 120 cm.

34

36 ABOVE Wall-painting from the Tomb of the Augurs, Tarquinia, showing funerary games in progress. In the centre, two wrestlers compete for prizes of bronze bowls, while on the left an umpire watches. He holds a curved stick (*lituus*) in his hand and behind him are a man wearing a red mantle and boots and a boy carrying a stool. On the right is a masked man, with *Phersu* written beside him; he holds a fierce dog on a leash, which is attacking another masked man who has a club in his hand. About 520 BC.

37 RIGHT Wall-painting from the Tomb of the Lionesses, Tarquinia, showing dancers and musicians at a banquet. The banqueters are painted on the side walls, and a huge mixing-bowl (*krater*) is seen in the centre of the back wall. The *krater* is flanked by musicians playing the double-flute and lyre, while dancers perform on either side. About 520 BC.

38 Painted pottery. *From left to right:*

a Etrusco-Corinthian jug (*olpe*) with polychrome and incised decoration in two friezes, representing a boar with lions above and a goat with panthers below. By the Bearded Sphinx Painter and made at Vulci, *c.*610–590 BC. H. 31 cm.

b Perfume-bottle in the form of a dead hare, derived from prototypes from a Greek city of Asia Minor. From Nola, Campania, 600–550 BC. H. 19 cm.

c Etrusco-Corinthian perfume-bottle in the form of a couchant doe, 600–550 BC. H. 5.5 cm.

d Etrusco-Corinthian perfume-bottle (*alabastron*) with polychrome painting representing a warrior, panther, birds and floral decoration. By the Pescia Romana Painter and made at Vulci, *c.*590–580 BC. H. 15.7 cm.

Corinth. As the sixth century progressed, an increasing amount of pottery was imported from Athens, and by about the middle of the century these Attic imports became the dominant influence from abroad. A sixth-century Athenian potter, Nikosthenes, actually copied the shapes of bucchero pottery and painted them in Athenian black-figure style for export to Etruria.

Here we may pause to describe the technique required to produce black-figured pottery. Clay with a quantity of iron oxide in its composition may be fired black or red, according to the temperature and amount of oxygen allowed into the kiln on firing. The 'paint' used by the Greeks to decorate their black-figured vases was in fact a purified and liquid form of the same clay used to create the vessel and, by a complicated sequence of temperature changes, together with the varying amount of oxygen allowed into the kiln during a single firing, Greek potters ensured that the body of the vessel was fired red, while the painted figures and other decorations were fired black. In black-figure technique, the figures are painted in silhouette with inner details incised or added in colour.

In Etruria, and probably at Vulci, there flourished a school of vase-painting making charming black-figured vases, termed the Pontic Class. These vases include both Greek and Etruscan bucchero shapes and were painted in black-figure technique, including brilliant touches of red or white, with friezes of lively animals, mythical or real, or scenes from life. Greeks from Asia Minor set up a workshop at Cerveteri which produced a fine series of water-jars, the Caeretan *hydriae*. These are well-balanced vessels with figures painted in black with vivid touches of reddish-purple and white. Few individual artists have yet been recognised among the indigenous pottery painters of the later black-figure style in Etruria; most important is the so-called Micali Painter, who worked at Vulci and produced vases with active and sturdy figures, sometimes representing mythical scenes but mingling these with moments taken from everyday life. The Micali Painter founded a school which continued the production of vases in the black-figure technique well into the fifth century BC.

39 RIGHT Black-figured pottery. *From left to right*:

a Jug (*oinochoe*) with two friezes of animals and birds. The jug belongs to the 'Pontic Class'; it is by the Paris Painter and was made at Vulci, *c.*550–530 BC. H. 29.5 cm.

b Caeretan water-jar (*hydria*) with a combat scene and lotus flowers and palmettes below. By the Eagle Painter, a Greek from Asia Minor who settled and worked at Cerveteri (Caere) or its port, Pyrgi. From Cerveteri, *c.*530–520 BC. H. 44 cm.

c *Hydria* with a scene of the laying-out of the dead and a winged horse and centaur below. By the Micali Painter, and made and found at Vulci, *c.*510–500 BC. H. 41 cm.

40 BELOW Bucchero vases of the 6th century BC, with roller-stamped and mould-pressed relief decoration. *Front, left to right*:

a Chalice, probably made at Tarquinia, *c.*600–575 BC. H. 14.25 cm.

b Jug (*oinochoe*), probably made at Chiusi, *c.*575–550 BC. H. 18.4 cm.

Back, left to right:

c Water-jar (*hydria*) from Chiusi, 550–500 BC. H. 54.5 cm.

d One-handled cup or dipper (*kyathos*), from Chiusi or Volterra, 550–500 BC. H. 19.7 cm.

e Jug (*oinochoe*), probably made at Chiusi, 550–500 BC. H. 32.5 cm.

Bucchero continued to be made throughout the Archaic period, but later it went out of fashion and production ceased. At the beginning of the sixth century, it was widely exported from Etruria around the shores of both the west and east Mediterranean, especially a popular two-handled form of cup (*kantharos*). Early in the century, many forms of bucchero continued those of the Orientalising period, but now the vases were often decorated with a roller-stamp which impressed repeating patterns into the clay while it was still wet. These patterns included mythical creatures, rows of animals or real events. There were centres of production of this ware at Tarquinia and Chiusi. During the latter half of the century, bucchero became heavy in appearance and loaded with mould-pressed ornamentation in low relief. This heavy bucchero was largely produced at Chiusi and Volterra. A speciality of Chiusi at this time was a tray-like form of bucchero brazier; this was probably made exclusively for funerary use and would be filled with a variety of small bucchero objects. At Cerveteri, braziers and large storage vessels (*pithoi*) were made of coarse clay and decorated

80

40a, b

40c–e

with friezes impressed with a roller-stamp.

With local resources of both copper and tin, the Etruscans throughout their history were skilled and inventive bronzesmiths, arousing the admiration of the Greeks. Kritias, an Athenian who lived at the end of the fifth century BC, wrote: 'their [the Etruscans'] bronzes of every sort for the decoration and service of houses are best' (quoted by Athenaeus, *Banquet for the Learned*, 1, 28b). The Archaic period saw rapid development of bronzework in Etruria, both in sculpture, as mentioned above, and in household bronzes, with a major centre of manufacture at Vulci.

Chariots were adorned with fine bronzework: a magnificent example with panels of repoussé scenes was found in a rich tomb at Monteleone, whose contents are now in the Metropolitan Museum in New York. Such chariots must have been used for ceremonial occasions and it may be that they were sometimes embellished with precious metal. Folding stools, some decorated with ivory, were now used in Etruria and became one of the insignia of Roman magistrates. Etruscan society adopted the custom of reclining on beds or couches at banquets. Many vessels of pottery and bronze for the service of wine have survived, and examples also appear in scenes, some reaching huge proportions. Arms and armour mainly followed Greek models, with the Corinthian helmet, bell corsel and greaves, though some Etruscan types persisted.

Among outstanding household bronzes of the sixth century BC are the tripod-stands which supported bowls for mixing wine and water and which were decorated with many ornamental figures. Incense-burners with beautiful figures at the base of the shaft were introduced. Unlike the Greeks, who lit their houses with oil lamps, the Etruscans generally used candles; candelabra first appear during the Archaic period, though they were to become more common in the following centuries. Polished bronze has a good reflecting surface and in the ancient world was often used for mirrors: bronze mirrors were introduced in Etruria during the Archaic period and usually have engraved designs upon the back – an Etruscan speciality – though occasionally examples were decorated in low relief. In

41 Bronze mirror decorated in low relief and with silver inlay in the border of palmettes and linked spirals. Details of the central field are finely engraved, and names are written beside the figures. The scene depicts Herecele (Herakles) abducting a lady called Mlakuch. This is an Etruscan name, unknown in Greek mythology. Said to be from Atri, Abruzzi, 500–475 BC. D. 18 cm.

42 ABOVE Bronze incense-burner made of several cast component parts. These include the base with three feet, modelled as lions' paws resting on small tortoises and surmounted by couchant lions, and the figure of a dancing girl supporting the shaft. A bowl in which incense was burnt was once set on top of the shaft. Made at Vulci, *c.*510–490 BC. H. 45 cm.

43 RIGHT Bronze bowl (*lebes*) used as a cinerary urn. The lid is decorated with figures of a man abducting a girl and the rim with four mounted Amazons, their bows aimed forwards or backwards in Scythian fashion. The frieze engraved on the bowl depicts Herakles driving away the cattle stolen by Cacus, and scenes at funerary games. From S. Maria di Capua Vetere, Campania, *c.*490–480 BC. H. 67 cm.

44 ABOVE Luxury goods of the Archaic period:

a (*back, left*) Imported glass perfume-bottle (*amphoriskos*) on a gold stand decorated with bands of filigree. About 500 BC. H. 9.4 and 2 cm.

b (*back, right*) Piece of amber carved in relief with a satyr and a maenad. Perhaps made in Campania, and said to be from Ruvo, Apulia, *c.*500–480 BC. H. 17.3 cm.

c (*front*) Ivory plaques carved in low relief with a lion attacking an ibex and a reclining satyr with an animal, perhaps a panther, below. About 540–520 BC. W. 10.5 and 11.5 cm.

45 Gold jewellery. *Clockwise, from top left:*

a Three pins, with heads covered in granulation and surmounted by globules. 550–500 BC. L. 5.8, 8.1 and 6.5 cm.

b Brooch (*fibula*), with a bow in the form of a winged chimera and a horse on the end of the catch-plate. About 525–500 BC. L. 6.8 cm.

c Circular ear-stud with patterns in gold wire, granulation and inlaid blue vitreous paste. 530–500 BC. D. 6.8 cm.

d Pair of cylindrical earrings, the ends closed with openwork rosettes and the sides decorated with rosettes, female heads, lions and ducks. From Chiusi, 550–500 BC. L. 2 cm.

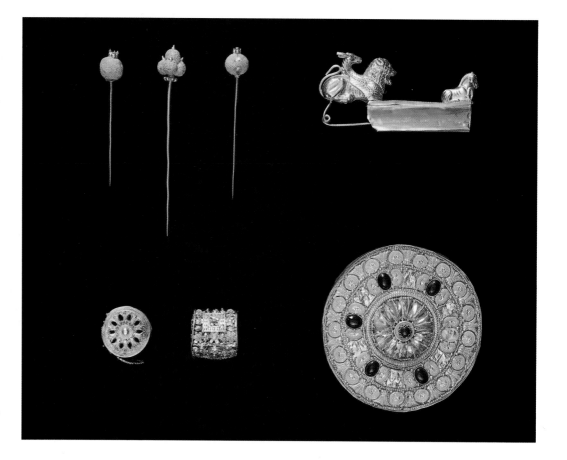

Campania, fine bronze bowls were used as cinerary urns; the inspiration for this form of urn came from Greece but was united in Campania with a typically Etruscan delight in figured ornamentation.

Etruscan jewellery of the Archaic period was more restrained than that of the previous era and included traditional Italian types as well as those of Greek inspiration. Delicate brooches (*fibulae*) continued Italian forms, and pins and earrings were worn, as well as large ear-studs, some inset with brightly coloured vitreous paste. Bracelets were worn, as were necklaces with glass and gold beads. Engraved gems, sometimes set in finger-rings, were introduced at this time.

Among luxury goods, small gold stands were made to support imported glass perfume-bottles. Ivory and bone were carved in low relief and the plaques joined to form small boxes, which were widely exported. Amber, perhaps carved in Etruscan Campania, was often used for pendants.

The Archaic period saw the greatest power and expansion of the Etruscans and their confidence is amply reflected in their art. Yet as it was ending, and the Greeks were about to face and emerge victorious from their great trial of strength with the Persian Empire, the Etruscans had already reached the zenith of their power and were to confront formidable foes both at sea and on land to south and to north.

5 The Classical Period 480–300 BC

The fifth century BC began with the revolt of the Greeks of Asia Minor from Persian domination, a struggle which led to the Persian invasion of Greece. Athens was sacked by the Persians but the Greeks won the great sea battle of Salamis in 480 BC, and in the following year beat the Persian army on land at Plataea. The Persians withdrew from Greece and the next decade saw the intellectual and artistic achievements of Classical Greece. It was said in antiquity that on the same day as the battle of Salamis, the western Greeks, led by the Corinthian colony of Syracuse, also defeated a barbarian host; the Carthaginians, allies of the Etruscans, had invaded Sicily with a large army but were defeated in battle near Himera.

This major reverse of her allies portended new dangers for Etruria, nor were these slow to appear. The Greeks of Cuma still felt threatened by the neighbouring Etruscan colonies in Campania and now asked help from Syracuse. Hieron of Syracuse sent a fleet to their aid, which defeated the Etruscans at sea off Cuma in 474 BC. From this time, the Etruscans could no longer assert their sea power in the Tyrrhenian Sea. Later in the fifth century BC the Syracusan fleet raided Elba and Corsica, and in 384 BC Dionysius of Syracuse sent a fleet into the Tyrrhenian Sea

and sacked the sanctuary at Pyrgi, carrying off great treasures.

This loss of sea power deprived the coastal cities of Etruria of open communication by sea with Greece and affected their trade with Athens; as a result, they may have suffered a minor economic recession. Certainly, power was beginning to move from the coastal cities, while those of the north were growing in strength, no doubt benefiting both from the continuing trade through the Etruscan ports of the upper Adriatic and even across the Alps into central Europe, and from the development of their agricultural potential.

During the fifth and fourth centuries BC, the Etruscans not only had to confront grave dangers at sea but also formidable attacks by land both in Campania and on the heartland of Etruria. In Campania the Etruscan colonies were cut off from Etruria by land and sea. Weakened and isolated, they were overrun by Italian Oscan-speaking peoples, including Samnite tribes; Capua was probably taken in 423 BC. The city-states of Etruria now faced both the rising military power of Rome in the south and the encroachment of Gaulish tribes in the north. The long struggle with Rome began with a series of campaigns around Fidenae (modern Fidene), which was taken by the Romans in 435 BC. There followed years of war between Rome and Veii, which culminated in an epic siege lasting for ten years. Livy (v, 1 ff.) tells us that the Faliscan peoples helped Veii in this crisis but, though they must have realised the potential danger, the Etruscan cities did not unite and come to the aid of the city. In 396 BC, Veii fell to the Romans; her inhabitants were sold into slavery and Rome annexed all her territory, breaching the southern boundary of Etruria.

Meanwhile, Gaulish tribes from north of the Alps were settling in the Po Valley, and it was said that an Etruscan colony was taken by them on the same day as the fall of Veii. Bologna and Marzabotto were overrun early in the fourth century, though the port of Spina survived and continued to import goods from Athens. Soon the northern cities of Etruria became involved. The Gauls crossed the Apennines in 391 BC and

46 Etruscan bronze helmet captured by the Greeks of Syracuse at the naval battle off Cuma in 474 BC, and dedicated at Olympia. The Greek inscription reads, 'Hieron, son of Deinomenes, and the Syracusans [dedicated] to Zeus Etruscan [spoils] from Cuma'. From Olympia, Greece, c.500–480 BC. H. 20 cm.

47 Limestone base of a tomb-marker (*cippus*) with scenes carved in low relief on all four sides, probably once surmounted by a stone sphere or cone. This scene shows young huntsmen returning from the chase with dogs at their heels and carrying hunting-hooks, a net and a dead hare which dangles from a pole carried across the shoulder. From Chiusi, *c*.480 BC. H. 45 cm.

the people of Chiusi asked help from Rome. The Romans sent ambassadors, who rashly joined the Etruscan army in the ensuing battle near Chiusi. In retaliation, the Gauls advanced on Rome, beat the Romans in battle, and took and burnt the city, except for the Capitol, before retreating home. The people of Cerveteri helped the Romans in this emergency by giving shelter to their priests, Vestals and sacred objects, a debt Rome repaid in later years.

Even after this disaster, the Romans soon again put pressure on the Faliscans and southern cities of Etruria including Civita Castellana, Cerveteri and Tarquinia. A bitter war was waged with Tarquinia between 358 and 351 BC. In 353 BC Cerveteri was granted a truce for one hundred years and perhaps given a form of Roman citizenship, and in 351 BC Tarquinia and the Faliscans sued for peace and were granted a truce for forty years, though shortly afterwards, the latter became subject-allies of Rome. The peace was observed for the forty years and during this time Alexander the Great led the

Macedonians and Greeks into Asia, conquered the Persian Empire and invaded India; the Etruscans were among the peoples to send an embassy to greet him on his return to Babylon, where he was to die in 323 BC. In Italy, Rome was drawn into the troubled affairs of Campania and fought a fierce war with the Samnites. When the truce ran out in 311 BC most of the Etruscan cities did combine and laid siege to Sutri, the Roman settlement or Latin colony that lay near the current boundary of Roman territory and that of Tarquinia. The following year, the Etruscans again tried to take the town but were defeated, retreating north through the great forest that still covered the Ciminian range of hills. The Romans then marched northwards and plundered the rich agricultural lands of Etruria; though the details are obscure, it is clear that they advanced into the area around Lake Trasimeno during the ensuing campaign. There was a battle and the Etruscan cities of Perugia, Cortona and Arezzo sued for peace and were granted truces for thirty years.

It was now clear that no single people or nation of Italy alone could oppose the Romans. The Samnites, defeated in their wars with Rome, marched north to form a confederation with the Umbrians, Etruscans and Gauls, but were again defeated in a decisive battle at Sentinum in Umbria during 295 BC. Now the Etruscan cities entered a final struggle for independence with many Roman incursions throughout their territories. In 283 BC an alliance of Etruscans and Gauls was soundly defeated in a battle near Lake Vadimo. By 280 BC, when the Romans were confronted by the landing of Pyrrhus of Epirus with a formidable army in the south of Italy, a general subjugation of Etruria appears to have been achieved, with all the Etruscan city-states now subject-allies of Rome. The Etruscans' loss of political independence was only a part of the growing domination of the Roman Republic over all the peoples of Italy.

By the end of the Archaic period, Athenian art had become the most important influence upon Etruscan sculpture and painting, but the transmission of ideas and styles became less rapid during the early Classical era. This may have

48 LEFT Bronze votive statuette of a warrior, cast solid. The shield and crest of the helmet, now missing, were made separately. The eyes were originally inlaid. The warrior once held a curved sword in his left hand and probably a spear in his right. He wears a scale corslet over a short tunic, and an Attic helmet with upturned cheek-pieces. From Falterona, *c*.420–400 BC. H. 32.5 cm.

been caused partly by an economic recession in Etruria, springing from the loss of contact with Greece via the Tyrrhenian Sea, but perhaps also from an Etruscan reluctance to follow the intellectual content and artistic innovations of the current styles of Athens. Thus the Etruscans were sometimes slow to accept the early Classical art of Greece and in both sculpture and painting Archaic forms lingered on well into the fifth century BC. Good examples of this slow development of some Etruscan art during the early fifth century are the charming scenes carved in low relief upon the base of tomb-markers (*cippi*) of 47 Chiusi or the tombstones (*stelai*) of Fiesole and Bologna.

Nevertheless, there were fine sculptural achievements in Etruria during the fifth century. These show a gradual acceptance of the severe style of early Classical Athens, with some idealisation of the human face and figure, now shown in relaxed poses, and an increased interest in anatomy, seen especially in nude male figures. Some poses express movement, with a left foot stepping forward; other standing figures have the weight of the body placed firmly upon one foot. These early Classical innovations were all more fully developed during the fourth century BC, when an artistic revival took place in Etruria.

Stone sarcophagi and cinerary urns appear at Chiusi and, during the fourth century, at Tarquinia, Tuscania and Vulci. Two outstanding sarcophagi from the same tomb at Vulci are now in the Museum of Fine Arts in Boston. Each has a married couple, clasped in each other's arms, carved on the lid, while on one of the chests scenes in low relief show the couple as they bid one another a fond farewell and ride off into the underworld, she seated on a cart and he mounted in a chariot.

Terracotta decorations from temples of the Classical period include several series of antefixes, some of heads but others with whole figures or pairs of figures. Revetment plaques often have moulded and repeating patterns of delightful floral motifs with lotus buds or palmettes. Notable sculptural achievements of the early fifth century BC include the fine terracotta plaque which once protected the end of the

49 RIGHT Hollow-cast bronze head of a young man, probably part of a votive statue. The strong features are capped by thick hair, modelled in curving striated locks. The eyes are sharply defined, the irises indicated by compass-drawn circles, and the beard is shown by fine incised lines. From an island in Lake Bolsena, *c*.375–350 BC. H. 21.5 cm.

50 Wall-painting from the Tomb of the Leopards, Tarquinia, showing a banquet. On the back wall, married couples recline on couches. They are served by boys, one holding a wine-jug, another a cup. Musicians painted on the side wall play the double-flute and lyre. About 480–470 BC.

central beam of Temple A at Pyrgi. This was modelled in high relief with overlapping figures shown in violent combat, depicting episodes in the Greek myth of the war of the Seven Against Thebes. The art of the Ager Faliscus was now closely akin to that of Etruria, and the terracotta fighting warriors from the Sassi Caduti temple at Civita Castellana may be mentioned here. The figures were once set above the sloping gable of the temple and are now displayed in the Villa Giulia Museum. Also from Civita Castellana and from Orvieto come beautiful terracotta heads, once part of the decoration of the temples. The modelling of a bearded head from the Via San Leonardo temple at Orvieto recalls the sculptural style of Pheidias of Athens (*c.* 490–432 BC).

During the fourth century BC, terracotta heads and some whole figures appear in votive deposits at sanctuaries in Etruria; like the votive bronze statuettes mentioned above, they were dedicated in gratitude to the gods. Among these is the 'Malavolta' head from Veii, which is now in

the Villa Giulia Museum. The head dates to the fourth century and shows the influence in Etruria of Polykleitos of Argos (*c.* 452–412 BC), but perhaps also that of contemporary sculptors of southern Italy.

The influence of the sculptural styles of Greece may also be seen in Etruscan bronze sculpture of the Classical period. A famous example is the large-scale statue of a warrior sacrificing, the so-called Mars of Todi, now in the Vatican Museums. This hollow-cast statue stands with the weight on the right foot and the hips thrust to that side; the warrior held a spear in his left hand and is shown pouring a libation with his right. The statue was probably made at Orvieto and, like the terracotta head mentioned above, shows the influence of Pheidias. A hollow-cast bronze head, once part of a statue, was also probably made at Orvieto. The style shows the influence of Greek Polykleitan forms but has typically Etruscan features like the rendering of the beard in a manner also found on terracotta heads.

49

Many bronze statuettes were dedicated at sanctuaries during the Classical period. One sanctuary was by a lake on Mount Falterona, a peak in the Apennines some forty kilometres to the east of Florence. After a chance find in 1836, about 600 bronze statuettes dating from the sixth to the third centuries BC were discovered here, as well as more than 2,000 other votive offerings. Many of these were lost and others dispersed to museums, including seven now in the British Museum. Among these is a graceful 48 statuette of a warrior, closely related in style to the Mars of Todi and also made in central or northern Etruria. A contemporary statuette of a 85 winged female figure, though an extremely Etruscan subject, is in a very Greek style and was probably made in a city of southern Etruria.

The tomb paintings of the fifth century BC continued many Archaic traditions, with the figures set in one plane and drawn with the heads in profile, the shoulders often frontal and the legs again in profile. Now scenes of banqueting were popular, with three couches shown on the back wall and serving boys and musicians on 50 each side wall. As in the celebrated Tomb of the Triclinium at Tarquinia, these figures are very carefully designed, with well-balanced patterns of movement and distribution of colours. These paintings of the early fifth century continue to express a full enjoyment of life, and include scenes of sports and games or acrobats and jugglers performing. Fewer tombs were painted during the second half of the century and generally these are of diminished quality. During the fourth century, however, several important technical innovations appear in painting in Etruria: artists were now able to achieve the impression of three-dimensional space and to draw figures in three-quarter views, their volume emphasised by shading and highlights. These developments are illustrated in the fine scenes on the Sarcophagus of the Amazons from Tarquinia, 51 now in Florence Archaeological Museum. The paintings have been attributed to a Greek hand, or that of an artist from a Greek city of southern Italy, but the sarcophagus was painted at Tarquinia. The beautiful paintings from the François Tomb at Vulci, now in the Villa Albani in Rome, also show the use of highlights, shading, mixed tones and well-designed contrast of light and dark areas (*chiaroscuro*). They are dated to the second half of the fourth century, a period when Vulci, together with other Etruscan cities, was again to be engaged in decisive conflict with Rome, and they reflect the mood of the time. The scenes depict an anxious scene of augury in which a member of the Saties family, dressed in a purple figured robe like the *toga picta* of a victorious Roman general, watches a servant perhaps about to release a bird and observe its flight; a violent episode of the ancient but more successful history of Vulci; Achilles' sacrifice of the Trojan prisoners; and the death struggle of Eteokles and Polyneikes. By the end of the Classical period, much of the confidence and joy

51 Painted scene on the Sarcophagus of the Amazons from Tarquinia, showing two Amazons attacking a Greek warrior. About 350 BC. (Florence, Archaeological Museum.)

52 LEFT Red-figured pottery. *Clockwise, from top left:*

a Vase (*stamnos*) with a horseman, Eros, and a winged [...]sa reclining below. By the Painter of London 484. Said to be from Vulci, *c.*400 BC. H. 35 cm.

b Faliscan mixing-bowl (*calyx-krater*) with Apollo sitting at the centre, surrounded by figures including the infant Herakles strangling the snakes. By the Nazzaro Painter. From Civita Castellana, *c.*400 BC. H. 50 cm.

c Faliscan jug (*oinochoe*) with a female head. Said to be from Vulci, 350–300 BC. H. 30 cm.

d Plate with a female head. Made at Cerveteri, 350–300 BC. D. 14 cm.

e Perfume-vase (*askos*) in the form of a duck. Made at Chiusi, *c.*325–300 BC, and found at Vulci. H. 15.25 cm.

53 LEFT Red-figured cup (*kylix*) with a scene of three women at their toilet. The central figure gazes at her reflection in a mirror, while to her right a woman lifts the lid of a casket (*cista*) in order to place a perfume-bottle inside. An oil-flask and scraper (*strigil*) hang on a hook nearby. Made in the territory of Chiusi. From Civita Castellana or Chiusi, 350–300 BC. D. 26.8 cm.

54 ABOVE RIGHT Bronze vessels for the service of wine, found together in a tomb near Bolsena. 350–300 BC. *From left to right:*

a Jug (*oinochoe*), inscribed *Larisal Havrenies suthina*, or 'The grave-gift of Laris Havrenie'. H. 31.5 cm.

b Ladle L. 40 cm.

c Mixing-bowl (*krater*) with the same inscription as the jug. H. 41.25 cm.

55 RIGHT Bronze handle from a vessel (*situla*) in the form of a youthful Herakles, who holds a club and looks at an apple in his left hand. A swinging-handle for the spouted *situla* would have passed through the ring at the top. 350–300 BC. H. 25.6 cm.

produced in Etruria and the Ager Faliscus, which was closely similar in artistic style. In Etruria, an early school flourished at Vulci which was much 52 influenced by Athenian prototypes, while by the end of the century a workshop had been set up at Civita Castellana, perhaps by an artist from Athens, and was producing ambitious works with many figures spaced over a wide ground. This workshop continued into the fourth century, making a range of beaked jugs, often painted with female heads flanked with palmettes, and a series of small plates, also with female heads.

Similar plates were produced by a red-figure 52d. e school at Cerveteri, while at Chiusi fine vases in title page sculptural forms were made, as well as vessels 53 decorated with elegant figures. A workshop at Volterra making vases in a somewhat less distinguished red-figure technique seems to have lasted at least to the end of the fourth century BC. Black pottery with added colour and so-called black-glazed ware was also produced in Etruria during the fourth century and continued to be made in the Hellenistic period (Chapter 6).

It is only possible to mention a few of the outstanding forms of utilitarian bronze objects of the Classical period. Helmets and armour broadly conformed with those of the Greek world, with Attic helmets and composite or scale corslets in use during the fifth century BC while 48 helmets adopted from the Gaulish tribes and corslets which were sometimes modelled with the muscles of the chest and abdomen were used by the Etruscans in the fourth century.

Much expense was lavished upon vessels for the service of wine at banquets, with storage jars (*amphorae*), spouted vessels and buckets (*situlae*), 55 mixing-bowls (*kraters*) and *stamnoi* adorned with beautiful figures forming handles and finely modelled handle-attachments and spouts. Sometimes sets of bronze utensils for the service of wine were placed as grave-gifts in a tomb and inscribed; such a set is the mixing-bowl, jug and 54 ladle from a tomb near Bolsena, with the inscription '*Larisal Havrenies suthina*' or 'Grave-gift of Laris [Lars] Havrenie'. A characteristic form of Etruscan wine-jug at this time had a pronounced 88 spout. There was a centre of manufacture of this

in life had departed from the tomb paintings, which now begin to show melancholy scenes of the departure of the dead for the underworld, or banquets there, sometimes in the threatening presence of demons.

The Etruscans were slow to adopt from the Greeks the technique of red-figure vase-painting. This involved the same methods of decorating and firing vessels as in that of black-figured pottery (see Chapter 4), but now the background was painted and fired black and the figures left unpainted, or reserved, to stand out in the red of the clay with the inner details painted usually in black. This technique permitted considerable new developments in the internal drawing of the figures, with more realistic details of anatomy and draperies. During much of the early fifth century, the Etruscans continued to use the black-figure technique, or to overpaint a black background with figures added in red, thus achieving the appearance of red-figured pottery without practising the new technique. During the second half of the fifth century and throughout the fourth, true red-figured pottery was type at Vulci and the jugs were widely exported both in Italy and even north of the Alps, where they were imitated by the local craftsmen in the current La Tène style.

Incense-burners with figures at the base of the shaft continued to be made. A most unusual bronze utensil of the fifth century BC is a large lamp in Cortona, made to hang from the ceiling and so decorated with cast designs on the underside. At the centre is the head of Medusa, while the encircling sixteen nozzles for wicks have winged sirens alternating with satyrs playing pipes. The manufacture of candelabra reached its apogee during the Classical period: the fifth-century Greek poet Pherekrates wrote, 'the lamp-stand [candelabrum] was Etruscan . . . for they were skilled and loving craftsmen' (quoted by Athenaeus, *Banquet for the Learned*, XV, 700c). The candelabra were made of several component parts cast separately, including a set of out-turned prongs set at the crown of the shaft, upon which the candles were fixed. The shafts were topped by statuettes, which present a wide variety of imaginary or realistic figures, among them satyrs and maenads, warriors and athletes, dancers and musicians.

Finely engraved mirrors have scenes in the contemporary style of drawing, many with inscribed names to identify the figures, which are shown in complicated and beautifully designed scenes of myth or real life. Most mirrors were now cast with a convex surface, which could reflect the whole face or head, and they were usually equipped with tangs which were set within handles of ivory or bone, some plain and others carved in low relief. Cylindrical bronze caskets (*cistae*) with engraved lids and sides and cast handles and feet began to be made during the fourth century, but reached their greatest production around 300 BC and in the following century (see Chapter 6).

Fine jewellery was produced in Etruria throughout the Classical period, and though Greek taste prevailed, Etruscan elements also survived. A group of jewellery from the tomb of a wealthy lady of Tarquinia includes a necklace with nine pendants or *bullae*. These *bullae*, usually round and hollow, and sometimes with

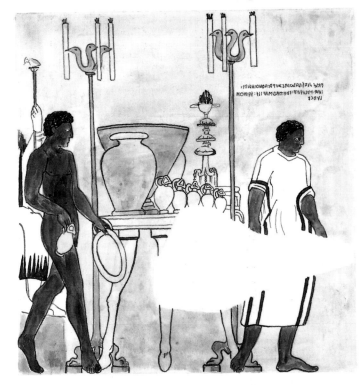

56 ABOVE Drawing of a wall-painting from the Golini Tombs near Orvieto, showing part of a banqueting scene set in the underworld. The serving boy holds a wine-jug and plate, and the table is laid with a mixing-bowl (*krater*), jar (*stamnos*), jugs and an incense-burner. Two tall candelabra, each with three candles, light the scene. 350–325 BC.

57 LEFT Statuette of a warrior which surmounts the shaft of a bronze candelabrum. Candles were fixed on the four prongs. Probably made at Vulci, *c*.475–450 BC. H. 21 cm.

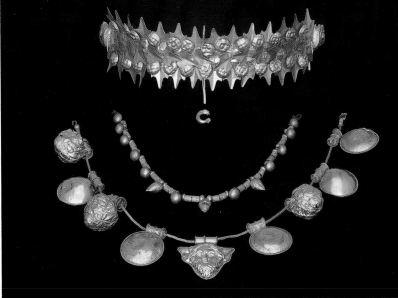

58 LEFT Gold necklaces:

a (*top*) Ribbon of plaited wire from which hang sixteen embossed heads of a horned god alternating with figures of sirens and acorns. From intersecting chains hang inverted lotus flowers and figures of sirens alternating with settings for onyx scarabs and amber. From coastal Etruria, *c.*480–460 BC. L. 27 cm.

b (*bottom*) A similar necklace with plain or granulated beads, rosettes, lotus flowers, acorns and lotus buds decorated with granulation. About 480–460 BC. L. 26.6 cm.

59 BELOW LEFT Gold jewellery, found together in a tomb near Tarquinia. About 400–350 BC. *From top*:

a Wreath with rows of ivy leaves and berries, and a satyr's head at either end. L. 31.75 cm.

b Earring with a lion's head at one end and decorative granulation at the other. D. 1.6 cm.

c Necklace of cylinders with pendant spheres and acorns. L. 28.7 cm.

d Necklace with nine hollow *bullae*, one of which is embossed with the horned head of a river god and three with the head of a youth. The plaited chain is probably Roman. L. 46.2 cm.

60 ABOVE

a (*left*) Gold earring made of thin sheet with embossed decoration and added filigree, rosettes and clusters of globules. 400–300 BC. H. 14.2 cm.

b (*right*) Terracotta votive head of a woman wearing similar earrings, a decorated head-band and a necklace with pendants. 325–300 BC or a little later. H. 23 cm.

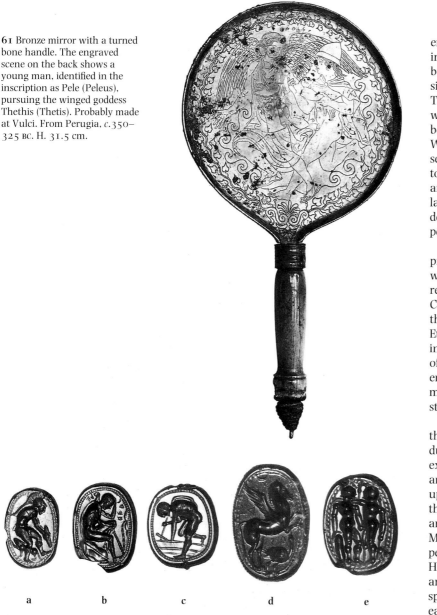

61 Bronze mirror with a turned bone handle. The engraved scene on the back shows a young man, identified in the inscription as Pele (Peleus), pursuing the winged goddess Thethis (Thetis). Probably made at Vulci. From Perugia, *c*.350–325 BC. H. 31.5 cm.

a   b   c   d   e

62 Engraved gems. *From left to right*:

a A warrior arming, *c*.480–450 BC. H. 1.4 cm.

b Herkle (Herakles) seated on a rock, *c*.400 BC. H. 1.6 cm.

c A craftsman using an adze, perhaps a scene of the building of the *Argo*. From Chiusi, *c*.400 BC. H. 1.4 cm.

d Pegasus and a bird, *c*.400–350 BC. The inscription is modern. H. 2.0 cm.

e Two warriors conversing, *c*.350–300 BC or a little later. H. 1.8 cm.

embossed or other decoration, were much worn in Etruria, even by animals. They must have been considered to have a religious or magical significance and were worn to avert bad luck. The Romans adopted the type, and *bullae* were worn by generals celebrating a triumph and by boys of good birth until they came of age. Wreaths formed of thin gold sheet cut to resemble leaves were now worn or carried to the tomb, as were necklaces, finger-rings, bracelets and several types of earring, including very large examples made of gold sheet elaborately decorated; they may be seen on some contemporary terracotta votive heads. 60

As was mentioned in the last chapter, semiprecious stones were engraved in Etruria towards the end of the Archaic period. This art 62 reached its highest achievement during the Classical period but did not continue long into the third century BC. These gems were used in Etruria as jewellery rather than as seals, and include many beautifully executed masterpieces of the fifth and early fourth century. Towards the end of the fourth century, the drill came to be much used, producing a rounded or 'globulo' 62e style.

The previously strong individual character of the art of Etruscan cities became less marked during the Classical era, when their artistic expression was largely based upon that of Athens and, during the fourth century BC, increasingly upon that of the Greek cities of southern Italy. By the end of that century, the conquests of Alexander had spread Greek culture round the east Mediterranean area, and during the following period, when his successors ruled the great Hellenistic kingdoms of the east, a common artistic style developed. As the power of Rome spread over the Greeks of Italy, Greece and the east Mediterranean, this common culture came to include Italy and was shared by the Etruscans, though they maintained some local characteristics, during the final centuries BC.

6 The Hellenistic Period 300–1st Century BC

By about 280 BC, all the Etruscan city-states had become subject-allies of the Roman Republic and their history became increasingly involved with that of Rome. The cities were allowed no political relations with other states and Etruscans were required to serve in the Roman army; however, the cities must have been permitted some local autonomy. Sometimes the Romans placed colonies in Etruria, like that of Cosa, settled in 273 BC on coastland once within the territory of Vulci. Roman power was enforced in Etruria when in 264 BC, after a social uprising at Orvieto, the Romans moved the population from their cliff-girt city to a less defensible site. During the third and second centuries BC Roman paved military roads were built across the region of ancient Etruria. These all led to Rome and often ignored old Etruscan settlements, but new focal points and towns grew up along their routes.

Certain events of the last three centuries BC

particularly affected the Etruscans. They fought as allies with the Romans during the last great Gaulish raid to the south of the Apennines, which ended in a decisive defeat of the Gauls near Talamone in 225 BC; following this victory, the Romans conquered the Gaulish tribes settled in the Po Valley. When Hannibal invaded Italy with his Carthaginian army during the Second Punic War of 218–201 BC and won a great victory by the shores of Lake Trasimeno, the Etruscan cities remained loyal to Rome. They contributed generously when Scipio Africanus called for supplies before sailing with his army to Africa, there to defeat Hannibal at the battle of Zama.

Little is known of the internal history of Etruria during the second century BC, for the interest of historians had turned to a wider sphere concerned with Rome's final destruction of Carthage and her wars with and ultimate

63 Painted terracotta sarcophagus of a well-to-do lady, whose name is written on the chest: Seianti Hanunia Tlesnasa. She wears a tunic (*chiton*) with a high girdle, a bordered mantle and jewellery including a tiara, earrings, necklace, bracelets and finger-rings, and holds a lidded mirror in her left hand. A skeleton of a woman about eighty years of age was found inside the sarcophagus, and a silver mirror, scraper (*strigil*), lidded box, flask and oval vessel hung from nails fixed in the wall of the tomb. From Poggio Cantarello, near Chiusi, *c.*150–130 BC. L. 183 cm.

conquest of the Hellenistic kingdoms of the Greek world. Yet we hear of a revolt of slaves in Etruria in 196 BC and agricultural decline later in the century. At the beginning of the first century BC, a federation of rebellious Italian peoples, including the Etruscans, fought the Romans in the Social War and, by 89 BC, they were granted Roman citizenship. Some Etruscan cities suffered severely in the vicious civil wars of the late Roman Republic before peace was finally restored by Augustus and the Imperial period began.

The process of assimilation of the Etruscans into the Roman world was now nearly complete; Latin was the generally accepted language and Etruscan art was merging with that of Rome. Yet men of Etruscan descent and Roman scholars and collectors remained interested in Etruscan antiquities.

As was noted in the last chapter, much Etruscan art of the Hellenistic period shared in the contemporary international culture of the Greek world, which was now increasingly dominated by the Romans, so styles and artists circulated with freedom. Yet many local artistic and social traditions were maintained in the Etruscan cities, as may be seen in the continued production of stone and terracotta sarcophagi and cinerary urns. The southern cities still generally practised inhumation, and many sarcophagi survive, principally from Tarquinia, Tuscania and Vulci. Though both inhumation and cremation were practised at Chiusi, and both sarcophagi and urns are consequently found there, cremation remained the traditional funerary rite in the north, and at some cities, like Volterra, it was used exclusively. The dead are shown singly or in couples on the lids of these sarcophagi and urns; occasionally, they are recumbent, as if in sleep, but most recline like banqueters. The heads are sometimes carved or modelled in the idealising manner of Hellenistic portraiture, but others are shown with a stark realism verging upon caricature. Many have their individual attributes carefully noted, and often their names are inscribed upon the

64

lid or chest. The inscriptions may include details of the deceased's family, age and career. Many of the terracotta sarcophagi and urns are painted in bright colours, which emphasise details of dress and jewellery, but others remained unpainted, like the elongated and schematically modelled examples from Tuscania.

63
65

The panels of the chests of these sarcophagi and urns were often carved or modelled in relief. Many show episodes taken from Greek epic or drama, some of which are repeated frequently, and it seems probable that the Etruscan sculptors, like the painters and engravers, had access to some Greek iconographic models or formulae. Sometimes the figures, or pairs of figures, are shown in relative isolation one from another, but as time progressed single figures become subordinated to the general scene, often in densely

64 *Nenfro* (a coarse-grained, local stone of volcanic origin) sarcophagus lid with the portrait figure of a woman carved in high relief. She holds a cup (*kantharos*) and ivy-tipped fennel-stalk (*thyrsus*), which, like the fawn-skin she wears and the fawn beside her, are attributes indicating that she was an initiate in the mysteries of Dionysos. From Tarquinia, *c.*250 BC. L. 221 cm.

interwoven groupings, an indication of the influence of the style of Pergamum, a Hellenistic kingdom in north-west Asia Minor. From the late fourth century onwards, violent moments of war and death were frequently chosen for representation, often with the figures of Charun with his mallet or a Vanth (an Etruscan Fury or demon of death) with a torch, both ready to guide the dead into the darkness of the underworld. Sometimes processions are shown, with the dead accompanied by relatives or their retinues approaching the door of a tomb. The production of cinerary urns at Volterra lasted well into the first century BC. They often show the influence of Roman art and symbolism, while Latin is used for some late Etruscan funerary inscriptions, like that on an urn from the Tomb of the Volumnii at Perugia.

During the Hellenistic period, the temples of Etruria were often furnished with revetment plaques of delightful repeating floral patterns, some of diagonally set palmettes and sprays of flowers, and showing pierced cresting rising above the gable, as may be seen from the temple terracottas at Cosa. Terracotta sculpture now filled the pediment; a beautiful example from a pediment group at the temple at Lo Scasato, Civita Castellana, is the dramatic head and torso of a youth, perhaps Apollo. This head is turned to the right and the youth has long curling hair, reminiscent of late portraits of Alexander the Great, probably by his favourite sculptor, Lysippos. Some almost complete pediment groups survive. These include the third-century group from Talamone, which depicts the myth of the Seven Against Thebes, now reconstructed in a Museum at Orbetello, and those from Civita Alba, near Sentinum in Umbria, dating to the second century BC, which show Dionysos discovering Ariadne on Naxos and the flight of Gauls from Delphi; these are exhibited in the Archaeological Museum at Bologna. These groups have many quite small figures, shown in intricate relationships one to another and with figures set high to indicate depth. The modelling achieves great elegance, the women sometimes shown nude as well as the men, and the figures depicted in supple, even exaggerated, poses,

65 LEFT Painted terracotta cinerary urn with the figure of a young man reclining upon the lid. He wears a white tunic (*chiton*) with a purple stripe, a mantle with a purple border and a gold finger-ring; and holds a bowl (*patera*) for libation, or offering to the gods. The name of a woman, Thana Ancarui Thelesa, is painted on the chest, which has a scene of five warriors. From Chiusi, *c.*150–100 BC. H. 74.8 cm.

66 ABOVE Front panel of an alabaster cinerary urn, showing a procession approaching a funerary monument. Two musicians are followed by horsemen carrying palm-fronds and a *fasces* (a bundle of rods with an axe, a Roman symbol of authority). Probably from Volterra, *c.*100 BC. H. 41 cm.

67 RIGHT Bronze votive statue of a young woman, wearing a sleeveless tunic (*chiton*) with a high knotted girdle and a mantle. It is uncertain what she once held in her hands, but perhaps it was a spindle and distaff. Said to be from near the sanctuary of Diana, Lake Nemi, Latium, 200–100 BC. H. 97 cm.

68 Drawing by S. J. Ainsley (1806–74) of the Tomb of the Typhon, Tarquinia. The walls and central pillar of the chamber are hewn from the rock and painted. On the pillar is a painting of a winged typhon, his legs formed of coiled snakes, who strains upwards as if to support a great weight. The remains of stone sarcophagi are shown lying upon the benches lining the walls. The tomb dates to 200–150 BC.

while the compositions as a whole strive to express emotion and to catch the dramatic moment.

As in the Hellenistic Greek world, an increased interest in portraiture is apparent, and in Etruria this may be seen not only in the heads of funerary figures, mentioned above, but also in terracotta votives and the few surviving large-scale bronze statues. A much-discussed bronze bust now in the Capitoline Museums at Rome, the so-called 'Brutus', shows a bearded man with fine, individual features. It has been suggested that this is a portrait of a distinguished Roman, made by an Etruscan sculptor around 300 BC. As the Hellenistic period progressed and the international styles of the Greek world were spreading, so too the arts of Etruria and Rome were converging: this is exemplified by the bronze votive statuettes of the last three centuries BC and by the Praenestine bronzes, mentioned below. There are two especially prominent series among the statuettes, one representing Herakles and the other sacrificing figures. The votive statuettes of Herakles, some of which are masterpieces with muscular bodies standing in sinuous poses while others have very schematic modelling, appear in Etruria and widely throughout Italy. The sacri-

ficing figures are common to Etruria and Latium and show both men and women, often in the act of pouring a libation and holding an incense-box. These also vary widely in quality: one particularly fine group is believed to come from the sanctuary of Diana at Nemi. They are related in style to a beautiful half-life-size statuette of a young woman said to be from the same site: her elongated figure, small head and supple pose are characteristic of the sculpture of the second 67 century BC. During the following century, the sculpture of Etruria was finally assimilated into that of Rome. A famous life-size statue from near Perugia, called the 'Orator' and preserved in Florence Archaeological Museum, presents a dignified man, perhaps addressing an assembly. It dates to the early first century BC, and the style recalls late Republican portraiture, while the inscription written on the hem of his toga is in Etruscan.

Painted tombs became more rare in Etruria during the Hellenistic period, and the practice seems to have died out by the beginning of the first century BC. Some of these tombs are relatively crudely decorated and others have only a frieze of arms or garlands, some accompanied by the painted names of the dead. Terrifying demons, coloured blue or green and holding mallets, flank doorways which are sometimes false and painted with architectural perspective. However, fine painting did persist during the second century BC, as is shown by the Tomb of 68 the Typhon at Tarquinia, named after the winged giant or demon depicted on the central pillar. His legs end in coiling snakes and his hands are raised, as if to support the painted cornice above; the torso is outlined but the bold foreshortening and modelling of the muscular body are mainly achieved by use of colour tones and shading. The dramatic pose of the straining torso and anguished turn of the head with tumbling hair recall the sculpture of Pergamum. In this tomb and some others, notably the Tomb of the Congress at Tarquinia, there appear on the walls solemn funeral processions of figures clad in togas, sometimes accompanied by attendants carrying the Roman symbols of authority; their heads are finely painted and come near to portraits. The interest in architectural details evident in these tomb paintings anticipates the Second 'Architectural' Style of wall-painting at Pompeii of the first century BC, while the composition of the processions looks forward to the reliefs of the Ara Pacis of Augustus.

Red-figured pottery was not made long after 300 BC, but vase-painting did not entirely cease in Etruria. The beautiful figure of a young huntsman in the tondo of a black bowl is painted in added colour in a technique closer to wall-painting than the usual decoration of pottery: it was probably made by a Greek working in southern Etruria, and must have been inspired by some large-scale painting. During the fourth century BC, local black Etruscan vessels, often cups (*kylikes*) and beaked jugs, had been decorated with added colour, predominantly white; early in the Hellenistic period, the Etruscans followed the workshops of southern Italy in producing so-called Gnathian ware, painting black-glazed pottery with added white, yellow and red, usually in simple patterns on cups (*skyphoi*) and jugs. At this time, so-called black-glazed pottery was widely produced in the Greek world, and there was a great centre of production in Campania. Black-glazed pottery was popular in Etruria during the fourth, third and into the second centuries BC and was made at several cities, including Volterra, where a fine blue/black surface was achieved. Vases were made with sculptured forms and often followed metallic prototypes; sometimes they were decorated in relief or with stamped patterns. Ornate vessels, usually for the service of wine, are found in the area around Lake Bolsena and were probably made there, so they are sometimes termed Volsinian ware. They imitate silver prototypes of south Italy and are frequently decorated in high relief and silvered, or covered with a slip (a thin coating of clay mixed with water) to imitate silver. These vessels date from the third and second centuries BC and represent the last major group of Etruscan pottery before the region was drawn into the economic and artistic sphere of Rome. However, it should be recalled that it was the potters of Arezzo who in the first century BC initiated the manufacture of the

69 Black bowl decorated in added colour and using shading, highlights and foreshortening of the figure. The scene shows a young hunter seated on a rock with a pair of spears in his hand and a dog by his side. About 300–280 BC. D. 18.5 cm.

70 ABOVE Black-glazed pottery. *From left to right:*
a Drinking vessel (*rhyton*), probably from the François Tomb, Vulci, 300–200 BC. L. 36.2 cm.
b Vase (*kantharoid-krater*) of the Malacena group (so called from the locality north of Siena of a tomb where much of this fabric was found). Made within the territory of Volterra and probably from the François Tomb, Vulci, 300–200 BC. H. 29 cm.
c Low bowl with one handle, of the Malacena group. Made in the territory of Volterra, 300–200 BC. D. 25 cm.
d Vase (*kantharos*) of the Malacena group. Made in the territory of Volterra, 300–200 BC. H. 13 cm.
e Bucket (*situla*) with reliefs below the handle attachments. From Vulci, 300–200 BC. H. 24.5 cm.

71 RIGHT Vase (*amphora*) with the head of an Amazon flanked by dolphins in relief. The head of Herakles appears below both handles, which have faces of maenads on their upper surfaces. Probably made near Lake Bolsena and found at Bolsena. 250–150 BC. H. 63 cm.

72 ABOVE Bronze lamp with three nozzles, surmounted by the figure of a winged youth holding a libation bowl in his left hand and pouring from a wine-jug held high in his right. He wears a high cap ending in a swan's head, which served as a hook to suspend the lamp. The underside of the lamp is decorated. 300–200 BC. H. 29.6 cm.

73

moulded, red-gloss Arretine pottery which was to become a favourite table ware of the Romans, widely exported and imitated around the Roman Empire.

There is no better manner of introducing a discussion of Etruscan bronze utensils of the Hellenistic period, and in this unique case those of perishable materials and iron too, than with a short description of the Tomb of the Reliefs at Cerveteri. The chamber of the tomb is characteristic of the early Hellenistic period and was cut into the rock below the surface of the ground, with two supporting pillars and niches for the dead around the walls. It is, however, unique in that its walls and pillars are covered in plaster, moulded and painted to resemble the familiar objects of Etruscan households. Here it should be recalled that few shelves or cupboards existed at the time, so household objects and personal possessions were habitually suspended from nails in the wall. The objects reproduced on the walls of this tomb include beds, a chest with a lock and a gaming-board, all presumably of wood; a purse and a satchel of leather; rope and slings of hemp

or some other material; pottery cups; bronze helmets and armour, trumpets, bowls and jugs, as well as knives, weapons and spits of iron.

The helmets shown in the tomb are of Gaulish type, but the Etruscans must generally have conformed with Roman military usage during the Hellenistic period. Among the household bronzes of the last three centuries BC, incense-burners continued to be used, now sometimes embellished with snakes or other creatures climbing up the shaft. Other examples lack shafts and are shaped like saucers with moulded rims. Few candelabra date from this period, but some pottery and bronze lamps are known. The game 72 of *kottabos* was introduced (see Chapter 7) and *kottabos* stands were made; also bronze bowls (*paterae*) with handles cast in the form of graceful figures. Portable bronze braziers continued to be used, and in both the Classical and Hellenistic periods were associated with bronze rakes and 74 tongs.

Elegant toilet equipment, mainly for women, was made in bronze as well as in precious materials. Hollow containers, usually cast in the form of heads of women or satyrs, were probably used for cosmetics. Engraved mirrors, now usually with cast handles, continued to be made 76 in Etruria and also at Palestrina in Latium. Lidded mirrors became fashionable; these had a polished disc, enclosed and protected by a hinged lid and sometimes a separate back; the outer 63 surface of the lid was sometimes embellished with an embossed sheet decorated with figures. As with the major arts, many everyday objects used by the Etruscans and the neighbouring peoples of Latium were becoming assimilated during the final centuries BC within the wider context of the current international Hellenistic style. This is well exemplified by the bronze objects made from the fourth to second centuries at Palestrina, where the craftsmen specialised in the production of engraved mirrors and caskets 75 (*cistae*). The mirrors follow the traditional Etruscan type with an engraved back but have a distinctive oval or pear-shaped form; sometimes they are accompanied by other bronzes of Etruscanising style, like a scraper (*strigil*) with the 75d handle cast in the form of a graceful girl. The

74 Bronze brazier for burning charcoal, with tongs and a rake. The shovel has a lion's head at the butt and that of a ram where the handle joins the scoop; above is a youth dressed in a hat and boots. It may have been used to carry lighted charcoal or for burning incense. D. of brazier 55 cm.

75 Praenestine bronzes. *From left to right:*

a and **b** Casket (*cista*) engraved with a scene of Bellerophon holding Pegasus, and beside it the cast handle with a girl holding a perfume-bottle and a young man with an oil-flask and scraper. About 300 BC. H. 48 cm.

c Mirror with an engraved scene of Ajax arming. From Palestrina, *c*.325–300 BC. H. 30.5 cm.

d Scraper (*strigil*) with a cast handle in the form of a girl holding a *strigil*. Found with **c**. About 300 BC. H. 41.2 cm.

76 Drawing of a bronze mirror with a cast handle. The engraved scene illustrates an Etruscan legend about Cacu (Cacus), who is seated playing a lyre. Beside him is the boy Artile with an open writing-tablet (*diptych*) in his hands. On either side, Aule and Caile Vipinas (Aulus and Caelius Vibenna) advance, either to eavesdrop upon Cacu or to capture him. From Bolsena, 300–200 BC. H. 30.8 cm.

77 Gold jewellery. *From top, left to right*:

a Earring decorated with bosses and globules and with a pendant female head and chains. From Perugia, 300–200 BC. H. 10.7 cm.

b Pair of earrings decorated with garnets and pendant cocks in white enamel. From Vulci, 300–200 BC. H. 3.8 cm.

c Earring with pendant of brown glass paste, and hanging chains. From Vulci, 200–100 BC. H. 4.5 cm.

d Pair of earrings with pendant winged figures. From Bolsena, 300–200 BC. H. 7.1 cm.

e Finger-ring with oval bezel and set with ten garnets and glass paste imitating onyx at the centre. From Chiusi, 300–200 BC. D. 3 cm.

f Hoop finger-ring ending in cylindrical ornaments, between which is a pivoting gem engraved with a dog. 300–200 BC. D. 2.1 cm.

g Pair of bracelets with embossed heads and figures, embellished with filigree. 300–200 BC. D. 8.7 cm.

cylindrical *cistae* have cast feet and handles, and are often minor works of art. The engravings on the lids and sides show inspiration from both Etruria and the Greek cities of southern Italy. On the Ficoroni Cista, now in the Villa Giulia Museum at Rome and perhaps the finest of all the Praenestine caskets, an inscription in archaic Latin reads, 'Dindia Macolnia gave me to her daughter'.

It was an appropriate present, for these caskets were used to keep a lady's toilet articles and have occasionally been found still containing them. They include multi-coloured glass perfume-bottles and wooden boxes, some finely carved in the form of a duck, the head of a horse or another motif, while the interior has compartments to hold powder, rouge or other cosmetics. Wood, bone or ivory combs have also been found in Praenestine caskets, as well as small pieces of sponge, which must have been used by ladies of the Hellenistic period to apply their cosmetics. Delightful boxes and other toilet articles were also made in gold or silver. The jewellery worn by ladies in Etruria during the Hellenistic period must have been very up-to-date and fashionable, for it sometimes appears indistinguishable from that of the Greek cities of south Italy and the wider Hellenistic world.

By the first century AD, Etruscan art and civilisation had merged with that of Imperial Rome but memories of the language and religion lingered on. Some country people of Etruria still spoke Etruscan during the second century AD. Julian the Apostate was accompanied by Etruscan soothsayers during his campaign in Asia, and an Etruscan offered to enlist the lightning to drive Alaric the Visigoth from the walls of Rome in AD 410.

77

Though the Etruscans learned much from the contemporary Greeks and shared many elements of daily life with neighbouring peoples, including the Romans, yet they were a distinctive 'nation' with their own language, religion and customs.

Language and writing

Etruscan does not belong to the great family of Indo-European languages, which includes Umbrian, Oscan and Latin in Italy, Greek, and Celtic, spoken by the Gaulish tribes. It is not known how long Etruscan had been spoken in ancient Etruria before the seventh century BC, when the alphabet was introduced and the language began to be written. Etruscan may have been long indigenous in Italy, perhaps belonging to a group of languages once widely spoken around the Mediterranean, or it may have been brought to Etruria by an immigrant population at an early date (see Chapter I). Apart from the sixth-century BC inscriptions on the island of Lemnos in the Aegean, no comparable language is known to us. However, Etruscan was influenced by neighbouring Indo-European languages; some Indo-European words entered the Etruscan vocabulary and Etruscan words were borrowed by adjacent Indo-European-speaking peoples.

The Greeks learnt the alphabet from the Phoenicians, adapting the use of some symbols to express vowels, and they brought their alphabet to Italy in the colonising age. In turn, the Etruscans adopted this Greek alphabet and altered it for their own use, dropping the letters B, D and O, for which they had no need, and adding the symbol 8 to express our letter 'f'. Like the early Greeks, the Etruscans usually wrote from right to left. It should be clearly stated here that the Etruscan alphabet, and therefore inscriptions when legible, can be read and that it is the language that is not fully understood.

For ordinary writing materials, the Etruscans used single or hinged tablets, which were waxed and inscribed with a sharp point or *stilus*, or wrote on long strips, or scrolls, of linen (the Latin *volumen*) with a reed or quill in black or red ink. They also had books of folded linen, one of which may probably be seen lying on top of the chest in

A	a
	(b)
Ↄ	c (k)
	(d)
Ⅎ	e
ꟻ	v
ꟼ	z
⊟⊘	h
⊙○	Θ (th)
	i
ꟼ	l
ᛗ	m
ᚼ	n
ꟼ	p
M	ś
ᗡ	r
?	s
↑ᛋ	t
V	u
Φ	φ (ph)
Ψ	χ (kh)
8	f
	1
Λ	5
X	10
↑	50
Ɔ ✱	100

78 The Etruscan alphabet, with modern transcription and pronunciation, and some Etruscan numerals.

79 Drawing of a bronze mirror with an engraved scene of a winged female figure holding an open scroll, upon which is written her name, Lasa, and those of two heroes, Aivas (Ajax) and Hamphiare (Amphiaraos), who are also identified on either side of her. It is likely that Lasa is foretelling the death of the heroes. 400–300 BC. H. 23 cm.

the Tomb of the Reliefs at Cerveteri. A few writing-tablets of ivory or wood have survived, but with one exception, an Etruscan book which was used for the bindings of an Egyptian mummy and is now in Zagreb in Yugoslavia, no linen scrolls or books have come down to us. The Etruscans, however, undoubtedly wrote books of several kinds; their religious texts were famous in antiquity and there is reason to believe they wrote history, works on agriculture and perhaps some drama. When the language became obso-

80 Bucchero cup (*kantharos*) with an inscription reading *Mi Repesunas Aviles*, or 'I belong to Aulus Repesuna'. About 600 BC. H. 12 cm.

81 BELOW Drinking vessel (*rhyton*) in the form of a mule's head. An inscription on the underside reads *Fuflunl Pachies Velclthi*, probably 'To Fufluns Bacchus at Vulci'. Probably from Vulci, *c.*400 BC. L. 19.25 cm.

lete, these texts ceased to be copied and recopied by scribes, and so this Etruscan literature written on perishable materials has disappeared.

About 13,000 Etruscan inscriptions have survived, however, since they were written on imperishable materials, including pottery, bronze, terracotta, stone or the plaster of the walls of tombs. Many of these inscriptions are short, and frequently repetitive. They may record the name of the owner of an object, the dedication of a votive offering, the name of the dead on a sarcophagus or cinerary urn, sometimes with details of the family, age, career or status of the deceased; they may identify the grave-gifts – *suthina* in Etruscan – for the dead, or name the figures on engraved gems and cities on coins. There are many inscriptions on bronze engraved mirrors, often identifying the figures represented: sometimes they are the Etruscan equivalents or adaptations of the names of Greek gods and goddesses or Greek mythical heroes and other characters; others are entirely Etruscan personages, like Mlakuch, Lasa, Thanr and Ethausva, or depict an Etruscan legend.

Long Etruscan inscriptions are rare: two important examples are the remains of the Etruscan linen book now in Zagreb, which has a religious text setting out the rituals to be offered to various gods on exact dates of the year, and the gold plaques from Pyrgi, two written in Etruscan and the third a rough translation in Phoenician/Punic language and script. These record a thanksgiving dedication to the goddess Uni or the Phoenician Astarte by Thefarie Velianas, the ruler of Caere. The plaques date to about 500 BC and are evidence for the close cooperation between the city of Caere and Carthaginians at this time.

The lack of comparable languages, the rarity

of bilingual records and the limited nature of surviving Etruscan inscriptions have hindered the study of the language. However, many Etruscan inscriptions are now understood, and the continuing study of Etruscan vocabulary and grammar shows a steady though limited progress.

The Etruscans were a highly literate people but the loss of their literature makes it impossible to evaluate all the ways in which they used this knowledge. They did much to educate the contemporary Italian peoples, passing the alphabet to many of their neighbours, including the Romans, Umbrians and peoples of the lower Po Valley.

Religion

In antiquity, the Etruscans were considered to be a uniquely religious people. They seem to have had a profound belief in the preordained and immutable course of divine will and that it was man's highest duty to seek the will of the gods and to conform to it, often with precisely fulfilled acts of worship, dedication or ritual. The Etruscans believed they had knowledge revealed by supernatural sources to help them discover the will of the gods by the interpretation of prodigies and by divination.

Such revelations were included in books such as the *Libri Tagetici* and *Libri Vegoici*, and the Etruscans also had other religious texts, the *Libri Fulgurales* and *Libri Haruspicini*, which dealt with divination by the observation of thunder and lightning, the flight of birds and the livers of sacrificed animals. The rules for such acts of divination were carefully set out. In the former methods, the priest or augur would stand facing south and note the qualities of the thunder and lightning, the type and number of the birds and the direction of their flight and their position in the sky. The dome of the sky was conceived as divided into sixteen parts, radiating from the observer, and these were considered the habitations of various gods; by a proper interpretation of the omen and the god concerned, the Etruscans believed the correct future action could be foretold. Similarly, the liver, used in divination, was considered as a microcosm of the universe

and the outer ring of a bronze replica of a sheep's liver from Piacenza is divided into sixteen parts, while there are forty spaces in all, in which the names of twenty-one gods are written. After the sacrifice of an animal, its liver would be examined by a haruspex, who would observe all its features in relation to the god concerned, and thus advise on future action.

At first many divine entities appear to have been conceived with little individuality and without human form. Some always remained anonymous, perhaps equivalent to the Fates. It was probably largely the influence of the Greeks that led to the personification and anthropomorphisation of divine beings in Etruria, and many Etruscan gods and goddesses came to be identified with those of Greece and Rome, including Tin or Tinia with Zeus (Roman Jupiter), Uni with Hera (Roman Juno), Menerva with Athena (Roman Minerva), Sethlans with Hephaistos (Roman Vulcan), Turms with Hermes (Roman Mercury), Turan with Aphrodite (Roman Venus) and Fufluns with Dionysos (Roman Bacchus). Greek myths are frequently illustrated in Etruscan art, often on the engraved mirrors with the names of the gods written beside them. There were also Etruscan deities not worshipped abroad, the chief of which was Voltumna.

Little is known of the rites performed at temples or sanctuaries, though a few scenes depict sacrificial animals being led to open-air altars. However, the vast number of votive

82 BELOW Votive terracotta models of parts of the body, 300–100 BC. *From left to right*: hand, internal organs, ears, eye, foot, breast. L. of hand 17.1 cm.

83 RIGHT Votive terracotta model of male and female figures seated on a bed within a temple or house, their heads covered with a mantle or bed-covering. Probably a marriage scene. 300–200 BC. H. 21.7 cm.

84 FAR RIGHT Black-figured cup with one handle (*kyathos*) showing a funerary scene of the laying-out of a man on his bed. The corpse lies on a mattress with a pillow, and a man and a woman stand at the bedside. On the left are eleven male mourners, and on the right ten female ones. The cup was probably made for funerary use, c.540–520 BC. H. 30 cm.

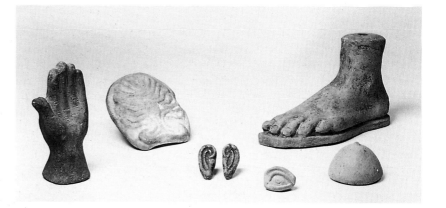

offerings so frequently mentioned above fully demonstrates that these sites were centres of religious devotion. Among the votive offerings dedicated at sanctuaries from the fourth century onwards are not only terracotta statues and 82 heads but also models of parts of the body, which must have been offered in the hope of a cure or in thanksgiving for a recovery and show the close association between religion and medicine. There 83 are occasional representations of marriage ceremonies. More often funerary rites are shown, 84 with scenes of the laying-out of the dead and 36 funerary processions, banquets and games.

It is difficult to interpret the Etruscans' conception of the afterlife. The cinerary urns in human form and tombs designed to resemble the interior of houses do seem to imply a belief that the dead, in some sense, lived on and needed familiar surroundings, while the joyous scenes painted in early tombs suggest the hope that the pleasures of life would be continued after death. In the fourth and later centuries, when the menacing 85 figures of the Etruscan demon or Fury, Vanth,

86 BELOW Bronze mirror with an engraved scene of Turan (Aphrodite) at her toilet. The goddess is elaborately dressed, wearing a necklace, earrings, tiara, *bullae* and bracelet. She is seated on a stool and gazes into a mirror held by a winged attendant, Achvizr. A second attendant is applying perfume to Turan's cheek with a long pin. 375–325 BC. H. 27 cm.

85 ABOVE Bronze statuette of a winged female demon or Fury of the underworld, called a Vanth. She wears a tunic with an overfold (*peplos*), buttoned at the shoulders, and holds a snake in either hand. Found near Mount Vesuvius, Campania. About 425–400 BC. H. 28.6 cm.

and Charun with his mallet appear, sometimes to escort the dead into the underworld or to threaten them there, it is difficult not to suppose the Etruscans had a despondent dread of death. Some cults – and both Orphic and Dionysiac sects existed in Etruria – may have taught that salvation could be sought through ritual. Since some Lasas (attendant divinities or nymphs) and demons associated with death hold scrolls in their hands, there may also have been some idea of judgement after death.

Government and social structure

The Etruscans were united by their common language and religion and each year it seems representatives from the twelve cities of Etruria met at the shrine of Voltumna, the Fanum Voltumnae, near Orvieto for a religious festival, games and a great fair, when mutual affairs could be discussed. However, the autonomous city-states of Etruria never formed a close federation and did not combine at crucial moments of their history, though they sometimes acted together in a common cause.

In early times each city-state was ruled by a king, called *lauchum* (Latin *lucumo*), who probably had both secular and religious authority. The early tombs testify to a very wealthy aristocratic class. The terraces of smaller tombs of the sixth and fifth centuries represent a more modest class, some perhaps merchants, and by the end of the fifth century it seems that political power had generally passed to oligarchies formed of well-to-do families, who provided an assembly and elected magistrates. Funerary inscriptions recording the careers of distinguished men provide the titles of some magistracies – *purth*, *zil* or *zilath* and *maru* – and we may conclude that a college or hierarchy of officials ruled in Etruscan cities, as at Rome. Certainly, the principal power remained in the hands of the oligarchic class of great families until the end of Etruscan independence, and the continuing deep division of the social classes in Etruria is shown by the civil strife at Arezzo in 302 BC, when an attempt was made to exile the rich and powerful family of the Cilnii (Livy, x, 3), the social uprising at Orvieto in 265 BC, and a revolt of slaves early in the second century BC. However, a general system whereby great families gave protection to their subordinates or clients in return for loyal support may well have made the situation of the underclass more tolerable. Beneath these classes were the serfs or slaves, who were sometimes freed by their masters, as we know from inscriptions. The Etruscans had many household slaves, like the well-dressed musicians, dancers, serving-boys or cooks whom we see in the tomb paintings. There must also have been many workers on the land, of whom we know little.

The continued pride of the great Etruscan families is clearly expressed in their funerary inscriptions and monuments. Family names were used by the seventh century BC, and subsequently family lineage was always traced through the male line, although the Etruscans gave aristocratic women a status and freedom unknown in Greek or early Roman society. They sometimes gave a woman the place of honour within a tomb, and often recorded the name of their mother, as well as their father, in funerary inscriptions. The wealth of Etruscan ladies is attested by their beautiful jewellery and luxury possessions, not least the engraved mirrors, which often give us a glimpse into a privileged woman's world. Many stories were told of the behaviour of Tanaquil, Tullia and other women of the Tarquin family, the Etruscan royal dynasty of Rome. They were said to have foretold the future, played a very active part in the affairs of state and dined with their friends. Unlike the secluded lives of contemporary Greek and Roman ladies, Etruscan women did dine with their husbands at banquets and attend public occasions, customs misunderstood and misrepresented by Greek and Roman authors but which seem very natural today.

War, economy and trade

The history of Etruria provides ample evidence that the Etruscans were formidable foes by sea and land: the Greeks recalled that they had terrorised the Greek sailors who first ventured into the Tyrrhenian Sea and the Romans remembered them as valiant soldiers. We can follow the development of Etruscan military

equipment, which has been mentioned in the foregoing chapters, but we know little about the naval or military organisation of the Etruscans. We have, however, a few scenes of naval engagements showing Etruscan warships with rams and manned with soldiers, ready to fight, as well as representations of hand-to-hand combat between warriors, armed in the contemporary manner. It is possible that in early times the authority of the kings could impose military discipline upon the army drawn from a city-state but that in later oligarchic times the great families would enlist their clients and other subordinates and thus fought as units, a type of regiment which could prove no match for that of the superbly organised armies of Rome.

In early times the economy of ancient Etruria was extremely soundly based; as the region evolved into city-states and agriculture and the exploitation of the mineral ores was developed, Etruria must have been self-sufficient in all essential natural resources, although gold had to be imported. Of the most important raw materials, the timber from the forests of Etruria was famous in antiquity and we hear of the export of grain as early as the fifth century BC. Though we have little information about the working of the land, except for a few scenes of harvesting, a model of oxen yoked to a plough and replicas of other agricultural tools, it is easy to believe that the Etruscans were good agriculturalists. Boundaries of estates were carefully maintained and a remarkable system for the drainage of water in underground tunnels, or *cuniculi*, was created. It may be that some Etruscans foresaw that the gradual cutting of the forests would result in the erosion of soil and the silting-up of valleys and the mouths of rivers; this was already occurring during the Etruscan period and resulted in swamps which encouraged the spread of malaria, no doubt partly responsible for the agricultural decline of the coastal cities. The mines of Etruria produced a variety of metal ores (see Chapter 1), but above all iron, which was smelted and exported in great quantities, probably beginning as early as the seventh century BC and continuing into the Hellenistic era. The contributions made by the Etruscan

87 Black-figured jug (*oinochoe*) of the 'Pontic Class', showing the preparations for a banquet in the upper frieze and a battle scene beside a building below. This scene includes a warrior wearing a Corinthian helmet with a high crest, a bell corslet and greaves. He has a round shield on his left arm, and is attacking with a spear. About 520–510 BC. H. 32 cm.

cities to Scipio's levy of 205 BC reflect both the fundamental economic potential of ancient Etruria and its current strengths: Livy records (XXVIII, 45) that the Etruscans sent grain, linen for sails, pine and hardwood for ship-building, iron, and manufactured goods.

Though raw materials must have provided the main exports of Etruria, bringing the Etruscans the purchasing power to attract so many goods from the east Mediterranean area and Greece over the centuries, as we have seen Etruscan manufactured goods were also exported. Outstanding among these were bucchero vessels and carved boxes of bone or ivory, but most important were the bronze utensils. Various types were exported to Greece and throughout Italy; one of the most popular and widely distributed of these was the wine-jug with a beaked mouth, which along with other bronze vessels for the serving of wine, and perhaps also the wine itself, was carried north of the Alps and there copied by local craftsmen.

Over a long period, the Etruscans must have conducted their trade by barter or other exchange systems, for coinage was not issued until a comparatively late date, perhaps early in the fifth century BC, and then only by some cities and in a sporadic manner. The coastal cities involved in international trade seem to have felt the greatest need for coins, in particular the city of Populonia. This city struck coins in gold, silver and bronze, often designed with the name of the city, Pupluna, and a reference to its major mining industry in the head of Sethlans (Hephaistos, Roman Vulcan), the smith-god, and a hammer and tongs. It seems that some Etruscan coins were issued for the payment of mercenaries in time of war. Unlike Greek coinage but like that of the Romans, Etruscan coins often have numeral signs of value; these show that the decimal system was used.

Dress

Like the Greeks and Romans, the Etruscans usually wore loosely draped garments, consisting of a tunic and an outer mantle, the Etruscan

88 ABOVE Bronze wine-jug (*oinochoe*) with a beaked mouth and a cast handle terminating in crouching felines on the rim and a palmette with volutes at the base. Probably made at Vulci, *c*.450–400 BC. H. 27.5 cm.

89 RIGHT Bronze vessels for serving wine, from a grave at Basse-Yutz, Moselle, France, *c*.425–375 BC:
Centre Two locally made flagons, imitating the shape of Etruscan wine-jugs with beaked mouths and elaborately decorated in Gaulish (Celtic La Tène) style. H. 37.6 and 38.7 cm.
Left and right Etruscan wine vessels (*stamnoi*), one with decorated rim and base, with cast handles ending in leaf-shaped attachments. H. 38 and 42 cm.

a   b   c

d   e   f

tebenna, made of linen or wool. The form of these garments, as well as the hair styles of both men and women, often helps to date the figures represented in art and to indicate their rank or profession.

Only a few examples of the changing fashions in Etruria, which are illustrated in the above pages, can be mentioned here. The heavy, perhaps woollen, plaid tunics and rectangular mantles worn in the seventh century BC were ₃₀ replaced during the Archaic period by a tunic (*chiton*) of a light material, perhaps linen, the _{back cover} ladies' long and sometimes belted and the men's quite short, occasionally reaching only to their ₉₁ thighs. Over these tunics, often embellished with coloured borders, the women are shown wearing coloured mantles, either falling down their backs, passing over their shoulders with slits for the hands or arms, or worn over the head, while the men sometimes have short mantles, which cross their left shoulder and pass under their right arm. A fine representation of the bordered mantle worn by men in Etruria during the late Archaic period is shown by a bronze statuette ₃₄ from near Prato: the young man's *tebenna* reaches down to the calf of his right leg and the hem curves upward on his left side. Both the *tebenna* of the Etruscans and the Roman toga were shaped

90 LEFT Etruscan coins:

a Gold coin, struck with a lion's head on the obverse. Uncertain mint, probably Populonia, *c.*500–300 BC. Max. D. 1.6 cm.
b Gold coin struck with a male head on the obverse and a bull on the reverse. Inscribed *Velznani* (probably Volsinii), *c.*300 BC. Max. D. 1.5 cm.
c Silver coin struck with a head of Menerva (Athena) on the obverse and on the reverse a star, crescent and the inscription *Pupluna* (Populonia), *c.*300–200 BC. Max. D. 2.3 cm.
d Bronze coin struck with a head of Sethlans (Hephaistos, Roman Vulcan) on the obverse, and on the reverse a hammer, tongs and the inscription *Pupluna* (Populonia). About 300–200 BC. Max. D. 2.6 cm.
e Bronze coin struck with the head of a negro on the obverse and an elephant on the reverse. Minted in northern Etruria, *c.*225–200 BC. Max. D. 1.8 cm.
f Bronze coin cast with the inscription *Velathri* (Volterra), *c.*300–200 BC. Max. D. 7.7 cm.

91 BELOW LEFT Detail from the Boccanera Plaques (Fig. 35). Paris, on the left, wears a short white tunic, a bordered shawl crossing his left shoulder and passing under his right arm, and a pointed hat, usually associated with priests. Hermes' white tunic has a stripe near the border and reaches halfway down his legs. Athena wears a long red tunic with bordered edges and boots with upturned toes.

92 RIGHT Black-figured storage vessel (neck-*amphora*) showing sporting events including a boxing match with two flute-players nearby. The amphora was decorated by the Micali Painter, and was made and found at Vulci, *c.*510–500 BC. H. 47 cm.

as a segment of a circle and the resulting curved hem contrasts with the horizontal hem of the rectangular Greek mantle or *himation*.

During the late Archaic period, the ladies of Etruria often wore a high, domed hat, called a *tutulus*. From the sixth century onwards, they tended to follow Greek fashion, like the Hellenistic tunic with a high girdle, but the aristocratic men and women of Etruria both retained local traditions in their dress during the Classical and Hellenistic periods and some of these were also followed by the Romans. It is often hard to suggest in which direction cultural currents were flowing, but it may be noted that Vel Saties, depicted in the paintings of the François Tomb at Vulci, wears a *toga picta*, usually associated with a victorious Roman general. While the musicians in the Tomb of the Shields at Tarquinia wear white mantles, which reach down to their ankles, the members of the Velcha family are

dressed in white cloaks with red or black borders, comparable with the *toga praetexta* worn by Roman magistrates and free-born boys.

Leisure

The banquets of the Etruscans, whether ordinary dinner parties or funerary feasts, have often been mentioned above. Many scenes show couples, undoubtedly husband and wife, reclining together upon a couch, while wine is served from jugs and lively dancers and musicians entertain the company. The dancers sometimes have castanets, and lyre-players are often shown, but the flute with two pipes was the favourite musical instrument of the Etruscans. It was said in antiquity that they boxed, kneaded bread and even whipped their slaves to its sound. The Etruscans were also credited in antiquity with the invention of the bronze war trumpet.

Many athletic sports were learnt from Greece and took place at festivals and fairs and at funerary games. Such sports included running races, the long jump holding jumping-weights, wrestling, boxing and throwing the discus. Equestrian sports included horse and chariot racing. Sometimes actors, jugglers and acrobats are depicted, and no doubt these performed at festivals and fairs.

The Etruscans also enjoyed hunting and fishing. In the paintings in the Tomb of Hunting and Fishing at Tarquinia a man aims a sling-shot at flying birds, while a boy dangles a hook and line over the side of a boat. Other scenes present pavilions or tents set up in the open air and, we may presume, in rural surroundings, for dead game hangs from the poles while men return from the hunt with dogs at their heels.

At home, the Etruscans played games involving lined boards, counters, knucklebones or their replicas, and dice; many of the latter have been found in their tombs and may also have been used in fortune-telling. During the Hellenistic period, Etruscan banqueters played the game of *kottabos*, already well known in the Greek world. In this game, the player threw the lees of wine in his cup at a detachable disc set at the top of a bronze stand; if he hit this disc, it fell and rang upon a large disc fastened below.

8 The Legacy of the Etruscans

The Etruscans were fortunate in the geographical position of their heartland and its rich resources. In the age when the Phoenicians and Greeks were colonising so many of the coastlands of the west Mediterranean area, the Etruscans were able to retain their lands, to organise the region into city-states, and to develop their natural resources, thus commanding a widespread trade which brought them great wealth. They were quick to acquire knowledge and skills from the high cultures of the east Mediterranean area and from the Greeks, including the art of writing, and during the seventh century BC they emerged as a Mediterranean civilisation.

As yet without foreign naval and military pressure encircling their heartland, the Etruscans reached their greatest power and expansion during the sixth century BC. The location of ancient Etruria gave a full opportunity of trade with the Greek world, and the Etruscans responded to this contact with a discriminating admiration for the contemporary arts of Greece. During the sixth and subsequent centuries, the Etruscans were an educating force among the Italian peoples and their influence reached beyond the Alps, but it was their close neighbours, the Romans, who most vividly recalled their ancient debt to them. In the years of their imperial domination of the Mediterranean world, the Romans remembered the Etruscans as cultivated neighbours in the days of the regal period and early Republic, and recalled that some of their hallowed symbols of authority and sacred rituals had come from Etruria. We know, too, that the Etruscans introduced the knowledge of writing to Rome, as well no doubt as many of their early arts and skills of craftsmanship and engineering.

As the numbers and pressure of the surrounding peoples of the west Mediterranean area and Italy grew in strength, the Etruscans were unable to withstand the Greeks at sea, the Gaulish raids from the north and, above all, the rising tide of Roman power. Whereas the genius of Rome extended the rights of the plebeian classes and admitted neighbouring peoples into Roman citizenship, thus ever enlarging her potential military might, the Etruscans maintained their traditional pride of family and their political organisation of autonomous city-states. The Etruscan cities did not unite when need arose, nor, it seems, did they learn to heal the divisions between the social classes. Though Rome remembered them as formidable foes, the Etruscans paid the penalty for these conservative attitudes and, like all the other peoples of Italy and indeed of the Mediterranean sphere, they were defeated and became assimilated into the Roman world.

Perhaps the greatest contribution of the Etruscans to the broad stream of European culture was their early example, which gave the first appreciation of Greek art to the Romans, who in the coming centuries did so much to preserve it for western civilisation. Nor were the artists of central Italy during Roman, medieval and Renaissance times unaware of the legacy of Etruscan art. Renaissance architects, sculptors and painters of Pisa, Florence and other cities clearly saw and valued Etruscan art and sometimes used the inspiration in their own work, so perhaps it was not entirely a coincidence that this revival of art flourished in the region that had been ancient Etruria. More recently, when Greek and Etruscan antiquities were found in quantity in Etruscan tombs, these became known throughout western Europe and profoundly influenced contemporary taste.

Modern travellers in ancient Etruria should be aware that it was the Etruscans who first set upon the landscape a form familiar to this day. They may visit Etruscan cities and towns, some covered by Roman and medieval remains, so that Etruscan work is scarcely visible, others now deserted and open to the eye, and they may wander in the evocative cemeteries and try to imagine the tombs as the Etruscans left them. However, the great surviving legacy of Etruscan art from their tombs, sanctuaries and other sites is now gathered in collections and museums in Italy, Europe and around the world. This diffusion of Etruscan objects, together with the current vast literature, has spread the knowlege of Etruscan culture more widely than ever and is continuing to enhance the appreciation of Etruscan civilisation.

Further reading in English

Boëthius, A., *Etruscan and Early Roman Architecture*, rev. ed. Harmondsworth 1978.

Bonfante, G. and Bonfante, L., *The Etruscan Language*, Manchester and New York 1983.

Bonfante, L., *Etruscan* (Reading the Past series), London and California 1990.

Bonfante, L. (ed.), *Etruscan Life and Afterlife*, Detroit 1986.

Brendel, O. J., *Etruscan Art*, ed. E. H. Richardson, Harmondsworth 1978.

Coarelli, F. (ed.), *Etruscan Cities*, London 1975.

Cristofani, M., *The Etruscans, A New Investigation*, trans. B. Phillips, London and New York 1979.

Haynes, S., *Etruscan Bronzes*, London 1985.

Macnamara, E., *Everyday Life of the Etruscans*, London and New York 1973, repr. New York 1978.

Pallottino, M., *The Etruscans*, rev. ed. D. Ridgway, Harmondsworth 1978.

Steingräber, S., *Etruscan Painting*, ed. D. and F. Ridgway, New York 1985.

British Museum registration and catalogue numbers

Front cover GR 1824.4–20.1 (*BM Cat. Silver Plate* 3)
Back cover GR 1850.2–27.1 (*BM Cat. Sculpture* D 1)
Inside front cover GR 1884.6–14.61 (*BM Cat. Sculpture* D 8)
Title page GR 1873.8–20.269 (*BM Cat. Vases* E 803)

Fig.
1 PD Cat. LB 23
4 a GR 1840.1–11.15 (*BM Cat. Vases* H 1)
  b GR 1924.5–16.1, GR 1963.5–23.1B
6 a GR 1894.5–7.3 (*BM Cat. Jewellery* 1373)
  b GR 1856.12–26.1367 (*BM Cat. Jewellery* 1355 *bis*)
  c GR 1976.2–5.16 (*BM Cat. Bronzes* 2044)
7 a GR 1968.6–27.1
  b GR 1849.5–18.30A and B (*BM Cat. Bronzes* 2751, 2710)
  c GR 1857.10–13.2 (*BM Cat. Bronzes* 2855)
8 a GR 1853.4–8.1
  b GR 1849.5–18.18 (*BM Cat. Vases* H 242)
10 PD Cat. LB 52
13 PD Cat. LB 40
14 PD Cat. LB 65
20 GR 1862.5–12.16 (*BM Cat. Jewellery* 1376)
21 a GR 1850.2–27.5
   b GR 1850.2–27.57
   c GR 1850.2–27.2 (*BM Cat. Sculpture* D 4)
22 a GR 1884.6–4.18 (*BM Cat. Jewellery* 1448)
   b GR 1852.1–12.3
23 a GR 1872.6–4.740 (*BM Cat. Jewellery* 1371)
   b GR 1840.2–12.1 (*BM Cat. Jewellery* 1372)
24 GR 1872.6–4.699 and 700 (*BM Cat. Jewellery* 1356–7)
25 a GR 1839.2–14.96 (*BM Cat. Vases* H 159)
   b GR 1839.2–14.89 (*BM Cat. Vases* H 171)
   c GR 1839.2–14.101 (*BM Cat. Vases* H 165)
   d GR 1836.2–24.398 (*BM Cat. Vases* H 198)
26 GR 1873.8–20.246 (*BM Cat. Bronzes* 357)
27 a GR 1921.11–29.1
   b GR 1925.4–21.1
   c GR 1867.5–8.882
   d GR 1859.2–16.39
28 GR 1867.5–8.374 (*BM Cat. Bronzes* 368)
29 a GR 1977.2–14.3 and 4
   b GR 1868.5–20.61 (*BM Cat. Bronzes* 363)
30 GR 1873.8–20.638 (*BM Cat. Terracottas* D 219)
31 GR 1853.6–4.1 (*BM Cat. Vases* H 245)
32 GR 1850.2–27.15B and 16 (*BM Cat. Bronzes* 434)
33 GR 1893.6–28.4 (*BM Cat. Terracottas* B 624)
34 GR 1824.4–97.1 (*BM Cat. Bronzes* 509)
35 GR 1889.4–10.1–5 (*BM Cat. Painting* 5a–e)
38 a GR 1836.2–24.258*
   b GR 1856.12–26.237 (*BM Cat. Terracottas* 1687)
   c GR 1814.7–4.490 (*BM Cat. Terracottas* 1690)
   d GR 1928.6–14.1
39 a GR 1978.5–2.1 (*BM Cat. Vases* B 54)
   b GR 1887.7–25.30 (*BM Cat. Vases* B 59)
   c GR 1836.2–24.159 (*BM Cat. Vases* B 63)
40 a GR 1867.5–8.846 (*BM Cat. Vases* H 186)
   b GR 1840.2–12.35 (*BM Cat. Vases* H 194)
   c GR 1873.8–20.356 (*BM Cat. Vases* H 208)
   d GR 1836.2–24.407 (*BM Cat. Vases* H 222)
   e GR 1914.2–20.1
41 GR 1772.3–4.7.4 (*BM Cat. Bronzes* 542)
42 GR 1848.6–19.11 (*BM Cat. Bronzes* 598)
43 GR 1855.8–16.1 (*BM Cat. Bronzes* 560)
44 a GR 1842.2–12.1 (*BM Cat. Glass* I 174) GR 1840.2–12.2 (*BM Cat. Jewellery* 1441)
   b GR 1856.1–3.46 (*BM Cat. Carved Amber* 35)
   c GR 1905.11–3.2 and 3
45 a GR 1872.6–4.821, 819, 820 (*BM Cat. Jewellery* 1351, 1350, 1352)
   b GR 1867.5–8.527 (*BM Cat. Jewellery* 1390)
   c GR 1881.5–28.2 (*BM Cat. Jewellery* 1419)
   d GR 1872.6–4.470 (*BM Cat. Jewellery* 1294, 1295)
46 GR 1823.6–10.1 (*BM Cat. Bronzes* 250)
47 GR 1865.7–29.2 (*BM Cat. Sculpture* D 18)
48 GR 1847.11–1.5 (*BM Cat. Bronzes* 459)
49 GR 1824.4–70.6 (*BM Cat. Bronzes* 1692)
52 a GR 1836.2–24.146 (*BM Cat. Vases* F 484)
   b GR 1888.10–15.13 (*BM Cat. Vases* F 479)
   c GR 1913.7–22.1 (*BM Cat. Vases* F 522)
   d GR 1838.6–8.149 (*BM Cat. Vases* F 522)
   e GR 1865.1–3.20 (*BM Cat. Vases* G 151)
53 GR 1892.5–18.2 (*BM Cat. Vases* F 478)
54 a GR 1868.6–6.2 (*BM Cat. Bronzes* 655)
   b GR 1868.6–6.4
   c GR 1868.6–6.5 (*BM Cat. Bronzes* 651)
55 GR 1824.4–46.12 (*BM Cat. Bronzes* 1249)
57 GR 1846.6–29.44 (*BM Cat. Bronzes* 592)
58 a GR 1856.6–25.17 (*BM Cat. Jewellery* 1461)
   b GR 1867.5–8.482 (*BM Cat. Jewellery* 1462)
59 a GR 1872.6–4.813 (*BM Cat. Jewellery* 2296)
   b GR 1872.6–4.505 (*BM Cat. Jewellery* 2207)
   c GR 1872.6–4.655 (*BM Cat. Jewellery* 1458)
   d GR 1872.6–4.643 (*BM Cat. Jewellery* 2271)
60 a GR 1841.3–1.5 (*BM Cat. Jewellery* 2256)
   b GR 1814.7–4.856
61 GR 1966.3–28.13
62 a GR 1867.5–7.424 (*BM Cat. Engraved Gems* 681)
   b GR 1814.7–4.1299 (*BM Cat. Engraved Gems* 769)
   c GR 1872.6–4.1156 (*BM Cat. Engraved Gems* 644)
   d GR 1772.3–15.406 (*BM Cat. Engraved Gems* 715)
   e GR 1856.12–26.1580 (*BM Cat. Engraved Gems* 817)
63 GR 1887.4–2.1 (*BM Cat. Terracottas* D 786)
64 GR 1838.6–8.9 (*BM Cat. Sculpture* D 22)
65 GR 1926.3–24.124 (*BM Cat. Terracottas* D 795)
66 GR 1925.2–18.1 (*BM Cat. Sculpture* D 69)
67 GR 1920.6–12.1
68 PD Cat. LB 1
69 GR 1855.3–6.16 (*BM Cat. Vases* F 542)
70 a GR 1884.4–9.8 (*BM Cat. Vases* G 26)
   b GR 1873.8–20.358 (*BM Cat. Vases* G 24)
   c GR 1836.2–24.322 (*BM Cat. Vases* G 30)
   d GR 1847.8–6.39
   e GR 1836.2–24.389
71 GR 1873.8–20.511 (*BM Cat. Vases* S 184)
72 GR 1824.4–54.25 (*BM Cat. Bronzes* 956, 2524)
73 PD Cat. LB 98
74 Brazier GR 1976.5–1.9; tongs GR 1975.7–11.1; rake GR 1975.5–17.2 (*BM Cat. Bronzes* 782.1); shovel GR 1824.4–98.35 (*BM Cat. Bronzes* 1227)
75 a, b GR 1884.6–14.33 (*BM Cat. Bronzes* 640)
   c GR 1873.8–20.104 (*BM Cat. Bronzes* 719)
   d GR 1873.8–20.2 (*BM Cat. Bronzes* 665)
76 GR 1873.8–20.105 (*BM Cat. Bronzes* 633)
77 a GR 1884.6–14.10 (*BM Cat. Jewellery* 2262)
   b GR 1884.6–14.3 and 4 (*BM Cat. Jewellery* 1677–8)
   c GR 1872.6–4.510 (*BM Cat. Jewellery* 2335)
   d GR 1872.6–4.561 (*BM Cat. Jewellery* 1845–6)
   e GR 1872.6–4.151 (*BM Cat. Finger Rings* 706)
   f GR 1872.6–4.26 (*BM Cat. Finger Rings* 342)
   g GR 1892.7–19.2 and 3 (*BM Cat. Jewellery* 2287–8)
79 GR 1847.9–9.4 (*BM Cat. Bronzes* 622)
80 GR 1953.4–26.1
81 GR 1837.6–9.79 (*BM Cat. Vases* F 489)
82 Hand GR 1756.1–1.1007; internal organs GR 1839.2–14.51; ears GR 1865.11–18.133 and 134; eye GR 1865.11–18.131; foot GR 1843.5–7.348; breast GR 1974.11–7.7
83 GR 1982.3–2.58
84 GR 1899.7–21.1
85 GR 1772.3–2.15 (*BM Cat. Bronzes* 1449)
86 GR 1847.9–9.1 (*BM Cat. Bronzes* 634)
87 GR 1926.6–28.1
88 GR 1867.5–8.725
89 *centre* PRB 1929.5–11.1 and 2; *left and right* PRB 1929.5–11.3 and 1929.5–10.1
90 a CM 1946.1–1.9
   b CM 1848.8–19.1
   c CM 1946.1–1.8
   d CM 1907.5–1.86
   e CM 1946.1–1.31
   f CM 1931.5–3.1
91 GR 1889.4–10.1 (*BM Cat. Painting* 5c)
92 GR 1865.1–3.25 (*BM Cat. Vases* B 64)

Index